ITALIAN PORCELAIN

The Faber Monographs on Pottery and Porcelain
Edited by W. B. Honey

*

GERMAN PORCELAIN *by* W. B. Honey
EARLY ISLAMIC POTTERY *by* Arthur Lane
ENGLISH DELFTWARE *by* F. H. Garner
COREAN POTTERY *by* W. B. Honey
FRENCH FAÏENCE *by* Arthur Lane
MEDIEVAL ENGLISH POTTERY *by* Bernard Rackham
WEDGWOOD WARE *by* W. B. Honey
GREEK POTTERY *by* Arthur Lane
FRENCH PORCELAIN OF THE EIGHTEENTH CENTURY *by* W. B. Honey
LATER CHINESE PORCELAIN *by* Soame Jenyns
EARLY STAFFORDSHIRE POTTERY *by* Bernard Rackham
NINETEENTH-CENTURY ENGLISH POTTERY AND PORCELAIN
by Geoffrey Bemrose
ENGLISH PORCELAIN OF THE EIGHTEENTH CENTURY *by* J. L. Dixon
ITALIAN MAIOLICA *by* Bernard Rackham
EARLY CHINESE POTTERY AND PORCELAIN *by* Basil Gray
WORCESTER PORCELAIN *by* F. A. Barrett
MING POTTERY AND PORCELAIN *by* Soame Jenyns
ITALIAN PORCELAIN *by* Arthur Lane
ORIENTAL BLUE-AND-WHITE *by* Sir Harry Garner

in preparation
ARTIST POTTERS IN ENGLAND 1890–1953 *by* Muriel Rose
ROMAN POTTERY *by* R. J. Charleston
BOW PORCELAIN *by* J. L. Dixon
LATER ISLAMIC POTTERY: PERSIA, SYRIA AND TURKEY *by* Arthur Lane
HISPANO-MORESQUE WARE *by* Arthur Lane
CHELSEA PORCELAIN *by* J. L. Dixon
SCANDINAVIAN POTTERY AND PORCELAIN *by* R. J. Charleston
ANCIENT AMERICAN POTTERY by G. H. S. Bushnell and A. Digby

*

OTHER TITLES TO FOLLOW
Edited by ARTHUR LANE

A. *Venice, Vezzi Factory*, 1720–27. *Mark 'Cf' incised.*
Ht. 4¾ *in.*
Victoria and Albert Museum
(*See p.* 12)

ITALIAN PORCELAIN

With a note on Buen Retiro

by

ARTHUR LANE

*Keeper of the Department of Ceramics
in the Victoria and Albert Museum*

FABER AND FABER

24 Russell Square

London

First published in mcmliv
by Faber and Faber Limited
24 Russell Square London W.C.1
Printed in Great Britain by
R. MacLehose and Company Limited
The University Press Glasgow

To
W. B. H.

FOREWORD

The neglect of Italian porcelain by students of art-history in view of the importance of the wares in the evolution of European porcelain is a piece of irony. No study adequate to the importance of the wares has ever been published, and a full survey has long been overdue.

Next to the Medici (which hardly comes within the collector's scope) there follow three groups—of the two or three Venetian factories and of early Doccia—still not properly classified. Even wares from the royal factory at Capo di Monte remain unsurely identified. Mr. Lane's task in classifying all these wares was arduous as well as rewarding.

W. B. H.

CONTENTS

FOREWORD   *page* vii

LIST OF PLATES   xi

ACKNOWLEDGEMENTS   xiii

INTRODUCTION   xv

1. THE MEDICI PORCELAIN (1575–87) AND OTHER

    EARLY EXPERIMENTS   1

2. VENICE: THE VEZZI FACTORY   8

3. LATER VENETIAN FACTORIES   14

    VENICE: N. F. HEWELCKE FACTORY   16

    VENICE: COZZI FACTORY   16

    LE NOVE   20

    ESTE   25

    TREVISO   27

4. VINOVO (1776–1820) AND OTHER

    NORTH-WESTERN FACTORIES   29

5. DOCCIA   32

6. THE BOURBON FACTORIES   45

    CAPODIMONTE   46

    BUEN RETIRO   52

    NAPLES: THE ROYAL FACTORY   57

MARKS   65

SELECT BIBLIOGRAPHY   74

INDEX   77

PLATES   *at the end of the book*

ILLUSTRATIONS

COLOUR PLATES

A. VENICE (VEZZI) TEA-POT   *frontispiece*

B. DOCCIA PLATE   *facing page* 36

C. DOCCIA FIGURE   *facing page* 42

D. CAPODIMONTE GROUP   *facing page* 50

MONOCHROME PLATES
after page 80

1–4. MEDICI PORCELAIN

5–13. VENICE, VEZZI FACTORY

14–15. VENICE, HEWELCKE FACTORY

16–27. VENICE, COZZI FACTORY

28–39. LE NOVE

40–42. ESTE

43. VINOVO

44–63. DOCCIA

64–82. CAPODIMONTE

83–89. BUEN RETIRO

90–96. NAPLES, ROYAL FACTORY

ACKNOWLEDGEMENTS

The Author wishes to express his gratitude to the private collectors and the authorities of the museums named in the plate-captions, not only for permission to reproduce photographs, but also for help in other ways. The photographs on Plate 96 are by gracious permission of Her Majesty The Queen. Special thanks are due in this country to the Victoria and Albert Museum, the Fitzwilliam Museum, Cambridge, the Cecil Higgins Museum, Bedford, and Mr. David Goldblatt. At the Musée Céramique de Sèvres, M. H-P. Fourest and Mme. M. Faré have shown unfailing kindness in helping his studies. In Italy, Dr. Vittorio Viale and his staff made it a real pleasure to work in the splendid collections of the Museo Civico at Turin. The late Professor Nino Barbantini, whose book on the Vezzi factory remained unpublished at the time of his lamented decease, gave valuable advice; and in Milan Signori Sandro Orsi and Saul Levy were most generous in providing photographs and helping him to see interesting pieces in private collections. The chapter on Doccia owes much to the friendly co-operation of the Marchese Leonardo Ginori-Lisci, who has freely communicated information from his own research on newly discovered records of the factory. Thanks are also due to the Marchese Roberto Venturi-Ginori of Florence; to Dottoressa E. Romano of Naples; to Dr. Siegfried Ducret of Zürich; to Señorita Felipa Niño of the Museo Nacional Arqueologico, Madrid; to Mrs. A. W. Frothingham of the Hispanic Society of America; to Miss Louise Avery of the Metropolitan Museum, New York; and to Miss Yvonne Hackenbroch.

INTRODUCTION

European porcelain was essentially a cult of the eighteenth century, with its climax between 1720 and 1770. First Meissen led the fashion, with its boisterous late-baroque colour and the nervous vitality of figure-modelling carried out in 'hard-paste' material. After 1756 supremacy passed to Sèvres, whose sumptuous effects of painting in deep colour could only be obtained in the less plastic 'soft-paste'.

In a sense all porcelain made elsewhere than in these two factories could be described as experimental or provincial. Italian porcelain especially lacks the high technical accomplishment found in Germany and France. There were no rich native deposits of china clay for making hard-paste, and though Capodimonte for a time made soft-paste porcelain of quality befitting its royal patron, the other factories aimed less high and struck a compromise with their hybrid materials. Though many artists from Austria, Germany, and France helped to nourish its growth, Italian porcelain as a whole retained a slightly eccentric character which is always refreshing and often evokes the welcome memory of the Italian scene.

With the Medici porcelain Italy anticipated by more than a century any other successful attempt to make soft-paste porcelain in Europe. The Vezzi factory in Venice during its short life competed with Meissen and Vienna while the manufacture of hard-paste was still in its nursery stage. Hereafter begin the problems of identity among the other factories, in which it is hoped that this book may carry knowledge a little further than the stage it has so far reached. For though Italian (and even English) students have published the results of their devoted research among documents relating to the manufacture of porcelain in Italy, much is still to be learnt from close study and comparison of the porcelain itself. Professor Giuseppe Morazzoni's great work *Le porcellane italiane* has earned the gratitude of all those interested in the subject, with the lively erudition of its text and the copiousness and quality of its illustrations. But the pieces it illustrates are seldom explicitly discussed, and many of the attributions are inconsistent or demonstrably incorrect. Here some advances can be made. But certain problems may continue to defy solution—how to distinguish between the porcelain of Capodimonte and that of the same factory after its transfer to Madrid; how to detect the activities of the Doccia factory during the nineteenth century. And there will always be individual pieces on which the connoisseur can sharpen his wits. They are as likely to turn up in England as anywhere else.

1

THE MEDICI PORCELAIN (1575–87)
AND OTHER EARLY EXPERIMENTS

Marco Polo came home to Venice in 1295. It is said, and it may be true, that he brought with him the small white bottle of Chinese porcelain with *ying ch'ing* glaze preserved there in the Treasury of St. Mark's. He was certainly the first European to see Chinese potters at work, at a place he called Tingui in Fukien Province which he visited during his years of service under Khubilai Khan (1275–92). And in describing the strange Chinese ware as *pourcelaine* he gave that word a new sense, which gradually ousted the original meaning of 'sea-shells' or 'mother-of-pearl' which it had in Marco's own time and retained for some generations later.

Vessels undoubtedly of Chinese porcelain are mentioned among the possessions of French noblemen in the fourteenth and fifteenth centuries—the Duke of Normandy (1363), the Duke of Berry (1416), and King Charles VII (1447).[1] And in Italy, in 1461, the Doge Pasquale Malipiero of Venice received twenty pieces of porcelain as a gift from the Egyptian sultan Abulfet Hamet.[2] A similar gift was sent from Egypt in 1487 to Lorenzo de' Medici in Florence.[3] We read in Vespasiano da Bisticci's *Lives of Illustrious Men* (written 1482–98) of Nicolao Nicoli, a Florentine scholar of the fifteenth century who was so cultured that he ate from 'the most beautiful antique vessels, and in like manner the whole of his table was covered with vessels of porcelain'.[4] The fame of Chinese porcelain in Italy at this time was certainly greater than knowledge of the material itself, though this was common enough in Egypt, Syria and Turkey, countries with which Italian merchants had long plied a vigorous trade.

The translucent Ming porcelain, painted in 'blue-and-white',

---

[1] Davillier, *Les origines de la porcelaine en Europe*, 1882, quotes numerous documentary sources.

[2] Marino Sanuto, *Le vite dei Dogi*, in *Rerum Italicarum Scriptores*, 1783, XXII, p. 1169.

[3] Letter from Piero da Bibbiena to Clarice de' Medici, quoted by Fabroni, *Laurentii Medicis Vita*, p. 337.

[4] *Vite di uomini illustri del secolo XV*, ed. L. Frate, 1893, Vol. III, p. 92.

appeared to combine the characteristics of pottery and glass, materials in which Italian craftsmen had achieved great success by the end of the fifteenth century. The potters were most active in Florence and other cities of Central Italy, making the tin-glazed painted earthenware known as *maiolica*. In the full tide of the Renaissance they had abundant resources for design, but they were sufficiently conscious of the Chinese wares to adopt from them the ornaments which they called *à porcellana*, slightly-painted running bands of coiled foliage that resemble the Chinese mainly in the colour-scheme of monochrome blue.

Venice had meanwhile become famous for its glass. Here the Chinese ware attracted admiration by its translucent glass-like property; and here began those long-frustrated European attempts to discover the secret of its manufacture. Urbani de Gheltof has published a letter, purporting to have been written by one Guglielmo da Bologna from Venice in 1470 to a friend in Padua, which accompanied a bowl and a vase of 'transparent porcelain', said to be as fine as that 'from Barbary', and painted in 'appropriate colours'; they were made by the alchemist Maestro Antonio at his new kiln in the parish of S. Simeone.[1] This letter is now believed to be an invention of Urbani, as no one else has been able to trace it. But a more reliable document refers to 'seven bowls of counterfeit porcelain' (*porcellana contrefatta*) bought by Ercole d'Este, Duke of Ferrara, while visiting Venice in 1504. His successor Alfonso I of Ferrara was in 1519 unsuccessful in an attempt to engage the services of a Venetian who had sent him a small plate and a bowl of *porcellana ficta*. This artist may or may not have been the mirror-maker Leonardo Peringer, who in the previous year had declared to the Senate his ability to make 'porcelain of every kind, like that called Levantine'. Rare existing specimens suggest that the Venetian experiments were conducted with opaque white glass painted in enamel colours, and not with clay materials.[2]

The scene next shifts to Ferrara, where in 1561–2 Duke Alfonso II engaged Camillo da Urbino and his brother Battista to make both *maiolica* and porcelain. Camillo died from an artillery accident in 1567, and Battista ceased experimenting in 1571. Contemporary references suggest that vessels purporting to be of porcelain were actually produced, though none have since been identified, and there survives in the Archives at Modena a recipe, dated from Ferrara in

[1] G. M. Urbani de Gheltof, *Una fabbrica di porcellana in Venezia nel 1470*, Venice, 1878 (quoted also by Davillier).

[2] G. Lorenzetti, *Una fiaschetta veneziana di vetro 'lattimo' dei primi del secolo XVI* (Dedalo I, 1920, p. 248); R. Schmidt, *Das Glas*, Berlin, 1922, Fig. 56.

1583, which prescribes as their material a mixture in equal parts of the same white tin-glaze and the same fine clay as were used separately to make ordinary maiolica.

With the 'Medici porcelain' of Florence we escape from the realm of documents and conjecture and can point to surviving examples of the first soft-paste porcelain certainly made in Europe. From 1537 Cosimo de' Medici, through the female line a grandson of Lorenzo the Magnificent, had built up by ruthless methods an economically prosperous state. In 1570 he achieved his lifelong ambition of being crowned first Grand Duke of Tuscany, and from then till his death in 1574 he handed over most of the administration to his son Francesco (born 1541). Cosimo bought in 1550 the unfinished *palazzo* begun over a century earlier by Brunelleschi for Luca Pitti. With growing additions, it became the Grand Ducal Palace, though today it is called the Palazzo Pitti. Here he re-assembled the art-treasures that formerly belonged to the Medici family, and encouraged the arts new to Florence of tapestry-weaving, crystal-carving, and *pietra dura* mosaic. Francesco I de' Medici (Grand Duke 1574–87), less a man of action than his father, immersed himself in the recondite handicrafts pursued in the workshops built in the Boboli Gardens and in the new Casino di San Marco. This morose and sinister prince was undoubtedly the moving spirit in the project of making porcelain.

We first hear of it from Vasari (*Lives of the most eminent painters and sculptors*, second edition, 1568), in discussing the achievements of his pupil Bernardo Buontalenti, a versatile genius who supervised all artistic undertakings at the Florentine court. Vasari says 'in a short time he will be seen making vessels of porcelain'—implying that in 1568 none had yet been made. In 1575 Andrea Gussoni, the Venetian Ambassador to Florence, wrote that the Grand Duke Francesco had rediscovered the method of making Indian (i.e. Oriental) porcelain, that he had spent ten years before finding the secret, and that a 'Levantine' had pointed out the means of success. (Galuzzi, writing his History of the Grand Duchy in 1781, expands this to 'a Greek who had travelled in the Indies'.) The reference has some significance, for in the Islamic Near East a translucent ware resembling soft-paste porcelain had been made for centuries past, and the contemporary wares of the flourishing potteries at Isnik in Turkey must have been known in Italy. Buontalenti probably did not concern himself with the material, though he may have designed some of the shapes. Flaminio Fontana, of a well-known family who made maiolica at Urbino, was in Florence from 1573 and in 1578 received payment for firing twenty-five to thirty pieces of porcelain; and Pier Maria '*delle porcellane*' of Faenza may have worked on it while in Florence between 1580–89.

In 1587 the Grand Duke Francesco I died, being succeeded by his brother Ferdinando I (1587–1609). One Nicolo Sisti was mentioned as a maker of maiolica and porcelain in 1592 and (at Pisa) in 1619. And at a festival in the Palazzo Pitti in 1613 the guests were given tokens of 'Royal Porcelain' stamped with the Medici arms. But it seems fairly certain that the serious manufacture of porcelain lasted only from its discovery in 1575 till the death of Francesco I in 1587.

According to a recipe preserved in the Biblioteca Magliabecchiana in Florence, the body of the porcelain was a mixture in the proportions 12:3 of glassy materials and white clay (probably kaolin) from Vicenza. The glassy matter included white sand; a 'frit' prepared from rock-crystal; and the same composition containing calcined lead and tin as was used for a white glaze by the makers of maiolica. The transparent lead-glaze was applied after the wares had been painted and biscuit-fired.

In his catalogue raisonné of 1936 Liverani lists fifty-nine recorded pieces of Medici porcelain, of which fifteen were at that time un-located. One of the latter, a plate, reappeared subsequently and was sold in 1949 at Messrs. Sotheby's in London for £1100, finding its way to an American Museum. Apart from the fourteen unlocated pieces four only still remain in private possession.

Almost all Medici porcelain betrays its experimental character by some technical defect. The white material is rather thickly potted and apt to sag out of shape; it is translucent, and can have a yellow or greyish cast. The thick, glutinous glaze may be clear or hazy with minute bubbles, and often has a wide crackle. It leaves bare the edge of the footring and sometimes 'misses' small spots on the surface, where the paste turns pink. Occasionally the blue painting is deep and rich, with purple outlines; more often it tends to grey. A spouted jug in the Baron Maurice de Rothschild collection is the only piece painted in polychrome, with blue, green and yellow 'grotesques' outlined in purple.

Some of the shapes are quite simple—plates with a flattened rim and central boss, bottles with twin spouts for oil and vinegar, flattened gourds, tall bottles square in section, and trefoil-mouthed jugs. Others show the wiry elegance and fantastic attachments found also in bronze and maiolica vessels of the later High Renaissance—ewers with constricted necks, snaky handles, and grotesque masks in relief. None are of obviously oriental derivation, except perhaps the flat-rimmed plates and gadrooned dishes.

The painted designs fall roughly into two classes—those borrowed from the repertoire of the contemporary painters on maiolica, and those of a pronounced oriental character hitherto unfamiliar in Italian ceramics. A dish which has passed from Baron Lambert's collection to the Metropolitan Museum, New York, has painted in the centre the Death of King Saul, surrounded by the spindly 'grotesque' ornaments and cameos derived from the antique and disseminated by Raphaël and his followers throughout the decorative arts. This kind of ornament, which was particularly popular among the maiolica painters of Urbino, is shown in simplified form on the gourd in Plate 1A. Three large gadrooned dishes in Lisbon, Florence and Arezzo have in their central medallions painted figures of the Evangelists, taken from engravings by Aldegrever after Georg Pencz (1). On a fat ewer in Baron Robert de Rothschild's collection are 'grotesques' and the impaled arms as Grand Duke of Francesco I and his Duchess Joanna of Austria; this piece can be dated between Francesco's accession in 1574 and her death in 1578, when he lost no time in marrying his mistress the notorious Bianca Capello. Three bottles of square section bear the royal arms of Spain and Portugal—one is dated 1581, and it is on record that gifts of porcelain were sent to Philip II of Spain in 1577 and 1582. (Francesco also sent one piece as a gift to Duke Alfonso of Ferrara in 1575, asking in exchange a sample of the mixtures prepared there by Camillo of Urbino;[1] seventeen further pieces were sent in 1583 to Don Alfonso d'Este, the Duke of Ferrara's uncle.) A medallion in the Bargello at Florence bears the date 1585 (or 6) and a bust portrait of Francesco I in low relief—perhaps after a design by Pastorino, whose initial 'P' is seen on the shoulder.

Pieces with 'oriental' ornament far outnumber the others. That in Plate 2C is marked under the foot *Prova* ('test') and must be one of the earliest made. The design of pine-trees, deer and birds, and the panels round the neck, immediately call to mind the blue-and-white Chinese porcelain made in the reigns of Chia Ching (1522–66) and Wan Li (1573–1619). Also of unmistakably sixteenth-century Chinese derivation is a dish in the Metropolitan Museum, New York, with a broad frieze round the centre of rocks, trees, water-plants, and 'clouds', among which are two figures in European dress. But on another gourd (2) the decoration is of Near Eastern character, and bears a distinct resemblance to that used by the Turkish potters of Isnik. On other pieces the stems of foliage and flowers wind in gentle and often asymmetrical rhythm over the surface, growing as if naturally from roots at the base of the vessel (3). It has been suggested that these plant-forms are derived from those on Persian blue-and-white wares, but it is unlikely that any of these should have reached

[1] See p. 2. Camillo da Urbino died in 1567.

---

(1) *Plate* 4C; (2) *Plate* 3C; (3) *Plates* 2A, B; 3B.

Florence at this date.[1] In Egypt and Syria the potter's art was in full decline. Turkey remains the most probable source, though it must be admitted that the Isnik wares of the time were usually painted not in blue-and-white, but in vivid polychrome.

Eight pieces of Medici porcelain, all gourds or flasks, are without a mark denoting their origin. They include the trial-piece (1), and are evidently early, about 1575. The six balls of the Medici arms, each inscribed with a letter 'FMMED II' (Franciscus Medicis Magnus Etruriae Dux Secundus) appear carefully painted as a mark on the ewer with the impaled Medici-Austria arms, which must be dated between 1574–8. On the dish painted with the death of King Saul is an Arch-Ducal crown over the six balls, which are inscribed 'FMM' (the rest illegible); and on a small ewer in the Louvre are five circles inscribed 'FMMED'. The remaining pieces, which may perhaps be dated in the ten years 1577–87, have as a mark the dome of Sta. Maria del Fiore, the Cathedral of Florence, with or without the letter 'F'.

Two small bowls in the Victoria and Albert Museum form an unexplained appendix to the Medici porcelain (2). They are inscribed 'I.G.P.F. 1627' and 'G.G.P.F. 1638' respectively, and are both marked with a cross potent and a sign that may be intended to simulate a Chinese character. The bowls are extraordinarily light, having been pared almost to paper thinness on the wheel; the paste is translucent and yellowish against a strong light. Round the outside and inside of the earlier bowl is a frieze of birds on rocks with simple trees or plants between them, and a central medallion contains a ruin on a mound between trees. The painting, under the transparent glaze, is mainly in blue with darker outlines; but the tree-stems in the middle are in opaque yellow-brown; and the foliage and details on the birds are touched in with copper-green. The later bowl (3) is painted in deep cobalt blue alone, with darker outlines, and has in its central medallion a view of a city among trees and mountains. The outside has four sprays of hyacinth and four of other flowers, crossed by large serrated leaves. This plant decoration is undoubtedly derived from that on the Turkish wares of Isnik, and suggests that the bowls are related to a class of maiolica made at Padua in the first half of the seventeenth century, which borrows its designs from the same Near Eastern source. A dish of this maiolica in Vienna has a central medallion with a view of a city, rather like that on the porcelain bowl, Plate 4A, and bears the mark of a cross potent and the inscription 'I.G. 1629'. It thus appears

[1] Most of the surviving Persian blue-and-white wares date from the seventeenth century, and at present it is unsafe to assume that they were made in quantity during the sixteenth century.

(1) *Plate* 2C; (2) *Plate* 4A; (3) *Plate* 4A, B.

that two artists 'I.G.' and 'G.G.' of the same family made both the bowls and maiolica, the further initials 'P.F.' perhaps standing for '*Padovano fece*' (of Padua made it).

The Medici porcelain all has a faintly magic quality, due not only to its rarity and the mystery surrounding its origin. At its best the painting shows a sensitive touch and fastidious restraint that are most admirable (1); it seems as if, by some subtle intuition, just enough has been borrowed from the East to form the basis of a style new in European art. One would gladly know more about the 'Levantine' who helped in the discovery of the paste-composition; did he also have a hand in the painted designs, and could he have possibly been a Greek who had worked at Isnik? Had the manufacture outlived its founder, it might well have altered the whole course of ceramic history in Europe. For the art of painted maiolica had lost its novelty; from about 1570 the simply decorated white wares made first at Faenza became a fashion that passed to other countries besides Italy, and not till the second half of the seventeenth century did an interest in elaborately-painted pottery revive. As for soft-paste porcelain, there was a long interval before its manufacture was once more attempted—by Louis Poterat of Rouen, who received a patent in 1673, but whose work can with difficulty be distinguished from the later and more abundant French soft-paste porcelain made at Saint-Cloud.

Only two forgeries of Medici porcelain have been recorded. One is a cylindrical covered vase with two handles, and 'printed' (more probably stencilled) decoration in blue and the dome mark; it appears to be an early Doccia production similar to those in our Plates 44, 45. The dome mark has been fraudulently added to another eighteenth century Doccia plate. Davillier and Liverani list two unidentified small globular jars shown at the South Kensington Exhibition in 1862; they were painted in enamel colours, silver, and gold, with roundels containing cupids and female busts in sixteenth or seventeenth century style. One of these recently seen in London appeared likely to be independent enameller's work dating from the second quarter of the nineteenth century.

2

VENICE: THE VEZZI FACTORY

(About 1720–27)

Few European states can trace a history so distinguished as that of the Most Serene Republic. From the fall of the Roman Empire Venice remained sovereign in her own territory; as the conqueror of Byzantium and defender of the Greek Islands against the Turk she acquired almost legendary prestige. As late as 1713, through her plenipotentiary Carlo Ruzzini, she composed differences between the great European powers at the Treaty of Utrecht. But from then till the abdication of the last Doge before Napoleon in 1797 her political role was a minor one; outwardly a city of pleasure, glorified by the art of Tiepolo and Guardi, but inwardly concerned to avoid war and repair the decline in trade.

The administration remained efficient. In commercial matters the Cinque Savii alla Mercanza (Board of Trade) maintained close supervision of local industries, and made recommendations to the Senate on behalf of those that deserved encouragement. Attention was drawn to ceramics in general by the failure of the first Venetian porcelain factory in 1727, and from 1728 onward surviving state papers enable us to trace the history of its successors.[1]

But there is still much to learn about the first factory, that founded by Francesco Vezzi (1651–1740).[2] He was a prosperous goldsmith who, with his brother Giuseppe, had in 1716 bought for 100,000 ducats the privilege of ennoblement. In March 1719 Vezzi is known to have sought permission from the Council of Ten to visit Augsburg for two months on private business, and it may be inferred that through other dealings abroad he knew of the progress of porcelain-making in Germany and Austria. At Meissen in Saxony the Royal Factory had greatly increased its sales between 1711 and the death in March 1719 of J. F. Böttger, the discoverer of the process and the first director. In

---

[1] Published by W. R. Drake, *Notes on Venetian Ceramics*, 1868; C. Baroni, *Le ceramiche di Nove di Bassano*, 1932; and G. Morazzoni, *Le porcellane italiane*, 1936.

[2] The late Professor Nino Barbantini had discovered further documents which he had hoped to incorporate in a book on the factory.

Vienna, a patent for the monopoly of making porcelain in Austria had been granted in May 1718 to Claude Innocent Du Paquier and three partners, one of whom was a goldsmith named Christoph Conrad Hunger.

Hunger was the man responsible for betraying the closely guarded secrets of Meissen, first in Vienna, and later in Venice. He had not been employed at the Meissen factory, but in 1717 he had converse with Böttger, who is said to have talked too freely when drunk. Hunger himself had special knowledge of enamel colours, and also of painting in underglaze blue. By diplomatic invitation he went to Vienna in October 1717 and joined Du Paquier in his experiments. These were apparently not successful till the spring of 1719, when Hunger persuaded the kiln-master Samuel Stölzel to desert Meissen for Vienna, and Saxon clay from Aue in the Erzgebirge was used for the first time. In 1720 Stölzel returned to Meissen, after doing his best to wreck the Vienna factory, and later in the same year Hunger disgraced himself and also had to leave. His way to Venice may already have been prepared.

It is assumed that Vezzi began making porcelain with Hunger's help in or soon after 1720. By 1723 he had given up his goldsmith's business for this more genteel occupation, and invested 30,000 ducats in a Company whose members may have included the influential statesman Carlo Ruzzini.[1] According to verbal information received from Dr. Nino Barbantini, there are documents indicating that Francesco Vezzi transferred control of the factory to his son Giovanni, who was held responsible for a financial crisis that led to the closure and pulling down of the kilns at the end of 1727. In June 1728 a report by the Board of Trade to the Senate referred to a porcelain-factory then 'already started' in Venice; but in a proclamation issued by the Board a month later this reference was dropped, and general encouragement offered to anyone who would introduce the manu-facture of fine earthenware and porcelain. It seems clear that the Vezzi factory was regarded as moribund. Francesco Vezzi's will, made in 1739, directed that other shareholders should be reimbursed from his own fortune, and that his own shares of 30,000 ducats should be invested in public funds. Vezzi's son Giovanni was then in exile, presumably disgraced through the failure of the porcelain factory. On Francesco Vezzi's death in 1740 one Luca Mantovani undertook to pay 100 ducats annually to the brothers Ruzzini (the Doge's heirs), for the rent and goodwill of Vezzi's kilns, which stood on their property in the parish of San Nicolo. The unreliable Hunger had cleared out in good time, for in August 1727 he reached Meissen and

[1] He became Doge from 1732 and died in 1735.

9

informed the Commissioners there that the Venetian factory depended on the china clay imported from Aue in Saxony. In 1728 export of this clay was forbidden by the Saxon authorities.

In its seven years of existence the Vezzi factory made remarkable progress. The best pieces bear comparison with the contemporary wares of Meissen and Vienna, and share their unpredictable strangeness of shape and decoration. Though it varies considerably, the material is always a true hard-paste porcelain of German type; indeed, students of German porcelain sometimes attribute to Vezzi pieces which they find difficult to place elsewhere. The colour can be pure white, creamy, or slightly grey, and is very translucent. The glaze is clear and wet-looking, unlike the opaque glaze found on early Vienna porcelain, or the glaze hazy with minute bubbles sometimes seen on the wares made in Böttger's period at Meissen. It sometimes takes a brownish tone where it lies thick, as on the teapot in Plate 8c.

Identification of Vezzi porcelain is usually easy, as most pieces bear a factory-mark—'Venezia' written in full or in the abbreviations 'Vena', 'Va', in underglaze blue, in gold, or in enamel colours (usually red). The painted mark is often accompanied by capital letters or figures of unknown meaning scratched in the paste.

Among the earliest productions, standing apart from the rest, is an unmarked table-service of tureens, coolers and dishes bearing the arms of an unidentified bishop and border-decoration painted in thick, badly fired blue, green, lemon-yellow, and iron-red enamels with black outlines (1). The hard white porcelain has an uneven, lumpy surface and is heavily potted; the glaze does not cover the bases. The ungainly shapes presumably derive from contemporary metalwork. A primitive white figure of a clown on a low disc base, in the Victoria and Albert Museum, seems to be of the same material.

The simpler shapes include globular teapots, rather heavily made, and often showing a twisted 'wreathing' in the paste like that found in English Bristol porcelain; saucers and tall or short cups without handles, usually with a more roughly finished footring than similar cups made at Vienna and Meissen; slop-bowls, and smooth-sided tea-caddies (2). There are also small vases painted in underglaze blue. But in this early stage European porcelain had not yet emancipated itself from the shapes proper to work in precious metal, where decoration is largely in relief (it may be remembered that both Vezzi and Hunger had been goldsmiths). The characteristic octagonal teapots have moulded relief-decoration of baroque character which does not always leave enough flat space for the painted ornament with

(1) *Plate* 6B; (2) *Plates* 6A, 7A, 10–13.

which they were further enriched (1). Another kind of relief-decoration was suggested by the white Chinese porcelain made at Tê-hua in Fukien province (*blanc-de-chine*). The oriental prunus-sprays were sometimes copied literally on Vezzi cups and saucers, but they also formed a point of departure for fanciful *chinoiseries* and festoons (2), and even European heraldry. The cup and saucer in Plate 8B bear in relief the arms of Pope Benedict XIII Orsini (1724–30) and the devices of the Dominican Order—it perhaps came from a set made for the Dominicans of San Giovanni e Paolo in Venice. A unique large vase in the Fondazione Querini-Stampaglia is related to the octagonal teapots in its elaborate relief-work (3). There are some smooth broad-shouldered jars and covers in the Ravà Collection,[1] painted with flowers similar to those on the teapot illustrated in our Plate 7A. The gondola-lantern and cover in the Victoria and Albert Museum is apparently unique (4), though pierced porcelain lanterns in other shapes were made at Vienna. This elaborate piece has rather feeble caryatid figures of children supporting the columns, and on the teapot in Plate 9A are terminal figures in relief. But so far as is known the Vezzi factory did not produce many free-standing figures.[2]

It is probable that the earliest colour used for painting was a blackish or greyish underglaze blue, which appeared here at least as early as at Meissen. It was used especially for *chinoiserie* designs, adapted from contemporary Augsburg goldsmiths' engravings (4), and for sketchily drawn figures of birds among foliage on the cups and saucers. The blue is sometimes outlined in a thin bronzy gold, which has almost the appearance of 'lustre' pigment (5); and sometimes there are added touches of crude enamel colours. These came to include iron-red, a rose-pink derived from gold, purple, yellow, blue, transparent emerald, and opaque yellow green. Indeed, the factory could contrive all the colours it wanted. But there was difficulty in laying them on; a saucer dated 1726, and therefore late, still shows very thick, smeary enamel colours in its fanciful mock-heraldry (6). The thin iron-red lay smoother; some figures are painted in red hatched lines (7), and a very distinctive and charming Vezzi motive is that of cross-hatched leaf-work in red (8).

Simple-minded oriental motives of pagodas and palm-trees, with

[1] Barbantini, *Le porcellane di Venezia e delle Nove*, 1936, Figs. 41–2.
[2] A possible Vezzi figure is mentioned on p. 10. The figures of Chinese women with unfired painting illustrated by Barbantini, op. cit., Figs. 49–50 may actually be Chinese.

(1) *Plates* 7B, 8, 11C; (2) *Plates* 8A, 9A, B; (3) *Plate* 7B; (4) *Plate* 5; (5) *Plates* 5, 6A; (6) *Plate* 13B; (7) *Plate* 10B; (8) *Plate* 11C and *Colour Plate* A, *Frontispiece*.

queer long-necked and long-legged birds flying above, are painted in underglaze blue, in thin gold alone (1), or in enamel colours (2). There are cups and saucers with European heraldry—one set has on the cup the arms of a prelate, and on the saucer the monogram 'PO' which has been said to refer to Cardinal Pietro Ottoboni (1667–1740) (3)—one of the most cultured Venetians of his time, Ambassador of France at the Vatican, and patron of Corelli and Handel. The colour is mainly in gold with details in red laid over it—a colour scheme repeated on a bowl in Lord Spencer's collection, which is dated 20 November 1727, and must be one of the last pieces made (4). Thick, smeary colours are used for the flowers and landscapes with ruins sometimes painted on the globular teapots, and for the hunting-scene on a saucer illustrated here (5).

The most accomplished piece of Vezzi painting is the Venus and Cupid on a saucer in the British Museum, finely stippled in crimson monochrome, probably after a late seventeenth-century engraving (6). It has on the back in the same colour a calligraphic inscription '*Lodovico Ortolani Veneto dipinse nella Fabrica di Porcelana in Venetia*'. The late Professor Barbantini informed me that he had found this painter's name among the others, all Italian, who according to unpublished documents were employed at the factory. He is not to be confused with the younger Lodovico Ortolani who worked later at Nove and at the Cozzi factory (see p. 17). Two cups in the Correr Museum, Venice,[1] with stippled mythological subjects in red and gold, and red, black, and gold respectively, seem to be by the same hand; one bears the mark 'Venezia' in red. The cup in our Plate 10A is stippled in blue monochrome, with a tooled gilt border, after a series of seventeenth-century engravings by O. Fialetti entitled *Scherzi d'Amore*. It may also be Lodovico Ortolani's work, though the attribution of these unmarked cups to the Vezzi factory has been questioned. Painting of the same high quality, in very bright and gay enamels, is seen on the octagonal teapots which are the most charming of all Vezzi porcelain. The subjects of grotesque peasants and plump ladies in fancy dress seem to have been borrowed from engravings of earlier date (7).

It remains to be said that there exist forgeries of Vezzi porcelain and some fraudulently added Vezzi marks. They are not difficult to identify. In the Museo Civico at Turin and the Correr at Venice are fat

[1] Illustrated by Barbantini, *Le porcellane di Venezia e delle Nove*, Figs. 38, 39.

---

(1) *Plate* 9C; (2) *Plates* 11A, 13A; (3) *Plate* 11B; (4) *Plate* 12A; (5) *Plates* 7A, 12B; (6) *Plate* 10C; (7) *Plate* 11C and *Colour Plate* A.

coffee-pots of smooth, simple shape, clumsily made of white earthen-ware; they have armorials and allegorical subjects badly painted in crimson, and absurdly flourished 'Vena' marks in crimson and gold.[1] Professor Barbantini had a genuine Le Nove jug (like our Plate 34A) to which polychrome painting of lovers in a landscape and the 'Vena' mark had been added in modern times. The mark 'Vena' in unfired gold has been added to the Doccia piece in our Plate 50B. A cup with the arms of Benedict XIII, like our Plate 8B, is shown at Turin with a later Doccia saucer, both with added painted decoration.[2] Needless to say, a good deal of porcelain made at Doccia, Meissen, and Vienna has in the past been incorrectly ascribed to the Vezzi factory. And mistaken attempts have been made to identify as Italian certain *blanc-de-chine* cups decorated in the raised and tooled gilding associated with C. C. Hunger.[3] In Venice, as in Vienna, Hunger appears to have acted solely as the 'arcanist' who applied the secret formula of composing the porcelain paste.

[1] V. Viale, *I Musei Civici nel 1932*, p. 6, Fig. 13. N. Barbantini, *Le porcellane di Venezia e delle Nove*, Figs. 65–68.

[2] N. Barbantini, op. cit., Figs. 30, 31. G. Morazzoni, *Le porcellane italiane*, Pl. LIV (as Capodimonte). The saucer, of typical grey Doccia paste, has relief-decoration on the back.

[3] N. Barbantini, op. cit., Figs. 20, 21. J. F. Hayward, *Viennese porcelain of the Du Paquier period*, 1952, pp. 118–9, suggests that a famous and unique covered beaker, decorated with figures of three Austrian Emperors in raised gold and enamel, should be regarded as a piece of Vezzi porcelain decorated by Hunger. I feel the previous attribution to Vienna is more probable in view of the subjects represented.

3

LATER VENETIAN FACTORIES

N. F. Hewelcke (1758–63); *Geminiano Cozzi* (1764–1812);
Le Nove (1762–1825); *Este* (from 1781); *Treviso* (about 1795–1840).

In 1727 the porcelain-factory of the Vezzi family came to a disastrous end. But such was the desire of the Board of Trade and the Senate to encourage local industries, that in the following year an inquiry was held and a Proclamation issued offering facilities to anyone who would start new factories for porcelain and *terraglie fine* (fine painted tin-glazed earthenware of the Delft type); or who would improve the standard of maiolica (painted tin-glazed earthenware as traditionally made). A similar Proclamation followed in 1732, soon after the accession as Doge of Carlo Ruzzini, whose interest in the Vezzi factory has already been mentioned (p. 9).

The responses to these Proclamations may be briefly listed before each factory is studied in detail.

In 1728 Giovanni Battista Antonibon opened a factory for *terraglie* at LE NOVE, a village whose name indicates its position on 'new lands' reclaimed from the River Brenta near Bassano, some 25 miles north west of Venice. In 1741 Pasquale Antonibon succeeded his father, and from 1752 he began experiments with porcelain. In 1762 the first samples were offered in Venice, and manufacture continued with some interruption until 1825. Workmen from Le Nove had great influence in spreading the secrets of porcelain to other factories in Venetia.

In 1738 the brothers Giovanni Andrea and Pietro BERTOLINI of Murano obtained privileges for making, 'in imitation of porcelain', vessels apparently of opaque white glass, with painted decoration. They never made real porcelain, and their work has not been convincingly distinguished from that of other contemporary glassworkers.

In 1756 the German Seven Years War began, and Frederick the Great of Prussia occupied Dresden. This crippled the neighbouring Royal Saxon factory at Meissen, and local retailers of porcelain went out of business. Two of them, Nathaniel Friedrich HEWELCKE and his wife Maria Dorothea, found refuge at Udine, in the Venetian *terra firma*, whence in December 1757 they addressed to the Board of Trade a petition for a monopoly of making porcelain for twenty years. By March 1758 their petition was granted, on condition 'that they marked the wares underneath with the letter "V" denoting Venice'. From March 1758 till November 1761 the Hewelcke operated at Udine, and thenceforward till about 1763 in Venice itself.[1] It appears that their efforts were not very successful; and in April 1763 the Senate extended permission to Pasquale Antonibon of Nove to make porcelain, observing how fortunate it was that competition should have arisen to spur on the two firms. But the Seven Years War ended in 1763, and the Hewelcke must soon have withdrawn to Dresden.

In 1765 their former associate the Modenese banker Geminiano Cozzi applied for the same privileges as the Hewelcke. He produced samples of a kind he had made for a year past, and adduced the telling argument that, unlike Vezzi before him, he could find all his raw materials in Venetian territory, and had no need to import them from Saxony. The Board of Trade and the Senate were so impressed by Cozzi's competence that they granted him a twenty years' privilege and financial support. The Board had earlier in the year conducted a tiresome inquiry into the affairs of Antonibon at Nove, whose workers were ill-disciplined and apt to wander off to join Cozzi's factory or to set up in practice on their own. Perhaps for this reason the Senate enjoined on the magistrates the task of stabilizing 'perfect concord between the two factories of Cozzi, porcelain, and of Antonibon, maiolica'. In spite of this broad hint to keep their activities distinct, the Le Nove factory went on making porcelain, and Cozzi from 1769 added to his own productions that of maiolica.

At Este, near Ferrara, runaway workmen from the Le Nove factory associated themselves with a local potter in 1765, but no identifiable porcelain was made until 1781. It was due to the researches of Jean-Pierre Varion, a Frenchman who left Le Nove in 1765, and after unsuccessful experiments elsewhere reached Este in 1778.

At Treviso the story is obscure; experiments were going on in 1759, but the only recognizable porcelain was made between about 1795 and 1840 in a paste obviously akin to that used by the Cozzi factory in Venice.

[1] Morazzoni says that experiments in Venice failed by August 1762. Urbani di Gheltof, without naming his source, says that the Hewelcke entered with Geminiano Cozzi into a partnership which ended in May 1763 (*Studi intorno alla ceramica veneziana*, 1876, p. 67).

ITALIAN PORCELAIN

VENICE: N. F. HEWELCKE FACTORY (1758–63)

Very few existing pieces can be attributed to the Hewelcke factory, and they probably all date from the years 1761–3 when the partners took up residence in Venice itself. The objects are marked with a letter 'V', firmly incised in the paste, and filled with a brownish-red enamel. The porcelain, perhaps made with clay from Tretto near Vicenza, is hard and slightly yellow in tone by direct and transmitted light. It has a thinly smeared, lustreless glaze, rather like wax in appearance, on an uneven surface. Typical shapes are shown in Plates 14, 15.

An opaque, shiny brownish red appears in the simple border-patterns, and on jugs or teapots it is used to pick out the modelled detail of spouts, of the scrolled loops connecting spout and body, and of the characteristic knob and tassel applied to the tops of the handles. The figures in seventeenth-century dress on the jug in Plate 14C might have been copied from an engraving by Jacques Callot; they are painted in a smeared brownish-purple—a colour used for outlines and shading of flesh-tones in the other pieces illustrated. Green and a bright dry yellow appear in touches, besides the purple and red. On the saucer, Plate 14B, an iridescent 'halo' has spread onto the surface round all the colours.

The plaque with an unidentified male portrait (I), perhaps moulded from a bronze, resembles the other pieces in material, and bears the mark 'V' in relief. Nothing is known of the modeller who signed the reverse with an incised cursive inscription 'Fortunato Tolerazzi Fece Venesia 1763'; but the date is a document for the continued existence of the Hewelcke factory in that year.

In material, shapes and decoration the wares all have a stunted and hesitant quality, much inferior to that of the other Venetian factories.

VENICE: COZZI FACTORY (1764–1812)

The Cozzi factory, situated in a palazzo on the Canareggio, in the parish of San Giobbe, was already at work for a year before obtaining its exclusive privilege from the Senate in August 1765. Cozzi may have learnt something from his association with the Hewelcke in 1762–3; but it is clear from the proceedings before the Board of Trade in 1765 that he benefited enormously through workmen who had deserted to him from Antonibon's factory at Le Nove. The paste first successfully used at Nove in 1762 was apparently discovered by one Pietro Lorenzi, who joined Cozzi in Venice in 1764, but returned to Nove in the following year. Cozzi may also have received advice from the

(I) *Plate* 15A.

16

geologist G. B. Arduini, who had surveyed the hills near Vicenza whence the essential white clays were derived. Among the painters who temporarily abandoned Antonibon for Cozzi was Lodovico Ortolani; his signature is known on a Cozzi saucer painted with flowers.[1]

Cozzi received state subsidies in 1765, and substantial loans, later converted into shares, from private backers. 16,000 ducats' worth of wares were sold in the first sixteen months after the privilege, of which two thirds were exported. In 1769 subsidiary kilns were started for making maiolica, and in 1781 Cozzi was granted 4,000 ducats to introduce the manufacture of cream-coloured earthenware of English type. The Senate intervened on Cozzi's behalf against his shareholders, against importations of foreign porcelain, and against exorbitant charges by the purveyor of clay from Vicenza. Not till 1790 did signs of financial strain appear; and the vigour of the factory, whose output must have been enormous, carried it through the French invasion of 1793 and the subsequent Austrian occupation until its closure in 1812.

Among the documents relating to the wares are notices which appeared in the *Giornale d'Italia* for 1765. They speak of cups, sugar-boxes, coffee-cans, figures, pagodas, snuff-boxes, and cane-handles. In the same year the Senate ordered for a state gift white and gilt tureens or compotiers, cups, coffee- and chocolate-pots. There also exists a catalogue of the wares dated 1783, which gives the names of various patterns and figures which can be identified.[2]

The factory-mark of an anchor, boldly drawn in iron-red, is almost invariably present on Cozzi table wares; exceptionally fine pieces have the anchor in gold. Figures and groups, on the other hand, are hardly ever marked; and unless peculiarities of modelling or colouring betray them, it is often difficult to distinguish them from the work of other factories—especially Le Nove, which used a similar paste.

The material shows little variation. It is hard,[3] distinctly grey in tone (but less so than Doccia), and has a glistening, wet-looking glaze.

---

[1] In the collection of Dr. Siegfried Ducret at Zürich; inscribed '*Nella Fabbrica Del Sigr: Geminiano Cozzi li 31 Maggio 1765 L.O.*' (See *Pro Arte* I, Nov. 1942, for illustration). The paste and handwriting are quite different from those of the saucer, Plate 10c, painted at the Vezzi factory before the birth of the second Lodovico Ortolani, who gave his age as 33 in the process before the Board of Trade in 1765.

[2] Published by Urbani di Gheltof, *Studi intorno alla ceramica veneziana*, 1876, pp. 69–75.

[3] Alexandre Brongniart (1770–1847), the famous Director of Sèvres, classified this and Doccia porcelain as 'hybrid soft-paste'. They are less highly fired than typical German and French hard-paste porcelains, but they contain kaolin from the Tretto pits near Vicenza, show a conchoidal fracture, and ring sharply when struck. We in England should certainly call them 'hard paste'; they are quite distinct from the French and English soft-pastes, and from those of Capodimonte, Naples, and Buen Retiro.

The vessels are usually heavier in construction than most German or English porcelain. Iron-red, violet, and a clear iridescent emerald green form a typical and piquant clash of colour; there is also a dull, heavy underglaze blue. The gilding, for which Venetian sequin coins were used, is very good and stands up thickly on the surface (1).

Early Cozzi table-wares show pronounced but rather fussy *rococo* details in shape (2). The handles are very eccentric, consisting often of overlapping leaf-forms or stems, and the pouting mouths of coffee-pots are unmistakable. There are plenty of applied flowers, leaves and fruit. Some early naturalistic flower- and fruit-painting is good (3); but the sticky enamel colours lend a slight air of roughness to the typical Italian Comedy figures and the society-groups in landscape (4). The enamels on German porcelain were smoother and more fluently worked. But a dated service of 1767 in the Correr Museum (5) has beautifully finished landscapes in iron-red monochrome,[1] and of the same high quality are some cups at Turin with mythological figures in iron-red and the anchor mark in red over-painted in gold. An especially elaborate plate dated 1780, which shows the influence of Sèvres in its dark blue border with rich gilding, is of special interest for its subjects; in the centre, Europa and the Bull, after Paolo Veronese; in the border-panels, miniatures after the masterpieces of Tintoretto and Tiepolo in the Doge's Palace at Venice (6). More ordinary Cozzi designs are the gardens with topiary and giant fore-ground flowers, called *à bersò* in the 1783 factory-catalogue (7); and the panelled, arched, or trellis patterns, sometimes containing miniature figures (8). The samples which Cozzi showed the Board of Trade in 1765 included imitations of 'Japanese'—more probably Chinese—porcelain cups; and *chinoiseries* of various kinds were a stock line, often recalling those on our own Lowestoft and New Hall wares (9). Almost identical motives were used at Le Nove. To shapes and decoration in the neo-classical taste of 1780–1800 Cozzi could contribute some pleasing and original variants (10); but his imitations of the Sèvres vases with coloured grounds were usually deplorable. 'Replacements' for broken services from other factories are known—for example, cups and saucers with battle-scenes in Capodimonte style. Cozzi porcelain is common in England though not often of the best quality.

Among the few marked Cozzi figures known to the writer are a

[1] The tea-caddy of this service is marked 'M.C.F. 8 Ag. 1767 Ven', incised.

(1) *Plate* 20c; (2) *Plates* 16–19; (3) *Plates* 18b, c; 19b; (4) *Plates* 17, 21a; (5) *Plate* 16; (6) *Plate* 21c; (7) *Plates* 20a, b; (8) *Plate* 22a; (9) *Plates* 23b, c; (10) *Plate* 22b.

rather feeble Chinese man and woman dated 1780,[1] and a bust of Antoninus Pius in the same late style as our Plate 27B. It is extremely difficult to distinguish between the work of Cozzi and the Le Nove factory, especially when, as so often happens, the figures are left uncoloured. But the Cozzi figures can often be recognised by the insipid meekness of expression on their faces, and a general weakness in the total composition of the groups. The feeling of Le Nove is more vigorous. Loose rococo scroll supports are found in early Cozzi figures and groups (1). Somewhat later comes a pyramidal arrangement on rockwork bases with a tree (*contadini con alberi* are mentioned in the factory-list of 1783). The same list mentions '*Endemioni*', presumably groups of Diana and the sleeping Endymion as shown in our Plate 25B. 'Pedestals', a separate item in the list, are circular, with masks or garlands in relief; sometimes they were fired in one piece with the group, but more often they were attached afterwards with cement (2). Similar pedestals were used at Le Nove. 'Pagoda' figures of squatting Chinese were mentioned in both the *Giornale d'Italia* of 1765 and the factory-list of 1783. Two fine examples are shown here (3), and an enormous one, some eighteen inches wide, is in the collection of Senator Aldo Crespi in Milan. The grotesque element again comes out in the figures and groups of dwarfs; the Alchemists (4) is a rare model, known also in painted white earthenware (*terraglia*). An allegorical figure of the Venetian Republic, *La Serenissima*, appears in several versions, naturally accompanied by the Lion of St. Mark (5), and in the Sèvres Museum are two bust portraits of Procurators of San Marco. There are brightly coloured miniature figures from the Commedia dell'Arte; scent-bottles in the form of swaddled infants, shoes, or negroes with detachable heads as stoppers (6). Some of the children suggest the influence of Sèvres porcelain (7). The figure of Hercules and the Nemean lion (8) is adapted from a Renaissance group outside the Palazzo Pisani in Venice, and classical busts such as that of Jupiter Ammon (9) conform with the cold neo-classical taste of the end of the eighteenth century. The colours on Cozzi figures include the characteristic brown-red, purple, and a rather unpleasant yellow-green. The flesh-tones are often filled in with opaque salmon-pink, smeared with red but not stippled. The dresses are commonly striped.

[1] Examples in the Musée Céramique at Sèvres, and Museo della Floridiana, Naples; marked with the anchor in gold and 'Vezia' or 'Venezia' on the front of the base. (Morazzoni, *Le porcellane italiane*, Plate CLIVa; E. Hannover, *Pottery & porcelain*, Vol. III, 1925, fig. 537.)

---

(1) *Plates* 26C, 27A; (2) *Plate* 27A; (3) *Plate* 24A; (4) *Plate* 24B; (5) *Plate* 26A; (6) *Plates* 25C, D, E; (7) *Plates* 26B, C; (8) *Plate* 27C; (9) *Plate* 27B.

Fakes of Cozzi porcelain are rare. But a figure of a seated harlequin with a pig has been seen with a Cozzi mark on the back of the base, though the paste and poor colours suggest that it is a nineteenth-century effort in the manner of Meissen (an unmarked piece in the Victoria and Albert Museum). An anchor in poor gold has been subsequently added to a genuine Doccia plate (1), and at Turin is a *trembleuse* cup and saucer of Saint-Cloud porcelain to which painted figures and a red anchor mark have been added in more recent times. Also at Turin is a genuine Cozzi covered bowl whose accompanying stand is an unmarked replacement of tin-glazed porcelain, perhaps made at Doccia.

LE NOVE (1762–1825)

At Le Nove near Bassano, Pasquale Antonibon, the proprietor of a flourishing maiolica-factory, began building a kiln for porcelain at the end of 1752. With him was Johann Sigismund Fischer of Dresden, who had apparently been employed as a painter at the Vienna porcelain factory in 1750, and who had certainly moved on from Le Nove to the Capodimonte factory by January 1754. In 1753 unsuccessful experiments at Nove continued with the help of an unnamed Frenchman, who may have been Jean-Pierre Varion.[1] By 1762 Antonibon had succeeded in making porcelain with kaolin from the pits at Tretto near Vicenza, his technical assistant being one Pietro Lorenzi. In the same year Antonibon submitted samples to the Board of Trade in Venice (the piece shown in Plate 28A may have been among them); and his request for a privilege and remission of customs duties was granted. But between 1763-5 Antonibon was ill; the factory languished, and many of his best workmen were forced to try their fortunes elsewhere. Some went to Cozzi's new factory at Venice; Varion tried to set up on his own at Bologna, and G. B. Brunello did the same at Este. In 1765 Antonibon recovered his health and instituted the proceedings before the Board of Trade mentioned above, with the result that many of his workmen returned. Unfortunately the Venetian Board of Trade grudged him support till 1773, when he was ennobled and retired from commerce to engage in local politics at Bassano.

Antonibon then leased his maiolica-factory to Giovan Maria Baccin, who worked it with success for about thirty years, and started a branch for cream-coloured earthenware of English type in 1784. But Antonibon's porcelain-factory apparently remained inactive till 1781, when he leased it to Francesco PAROLIN for twenty years. Parolin was

---

[1] For his further career, see p. 25.

(1) *Plate* 52A.

ably served by the modeller Domenico Bosello,[1] and by an eccentric painter named Giovanni Marcon. These two artists survived into the third period of the factory, 1802–25, when Parolin was succeeded as director by Giovanni BARONI. Through its chequered history the Nove factory was troubled by the desertion of workmen to start rival concerns; by the disturbances of Napoleon's invasion in 1796; and by the economic collapse of Venetia under subsequent Austrian misrule. It nevertheless produced some excellent porcelain, even after 1800.

The paste is virtually indistinguishable from that of Cozzi's porcelain, being slightly grey with a wet-looking glaze that develops a brownish tone where it lies thick. As Cozzi started with the help of workmen and stolen materials from Le Nove, it is not surprising that the colours used by both factories are virtually the same—the brown-red, violet and green in particular. But in the Parolin period and later, especially on pieces painted in the manner of Giovanni Marcon, some very individual colours were added. A soft grey-green contrasts with the emerald; a transparent rose-pink, derived from gold, offsets the iron red. Tooled gilding of very high quality is conspicuous on late Nove porcelain.

The factory-mark of a star with six points, usually in red or gold, was adopted from the Antonibon period (1762–73) onwards. It consists of crossed strokes, and does not have a solid centre like the star-mark of Doccia. The name 'Nove' appears incised in the paste on groups, and occasionally painted in gold on useful wares. Signatures of the painter Giovanni Marcon are found incorporated in the subjects as well as painted under bases. The initials 'GAB' or 'FAB' (Giovanni or Fabbrica Antonibon) appear in the design of useful wares of about 1762 or on bales of merchandise in a later group (|). 'G.B.' (Giovanni Baroni) is sometimes hidden in the design on wares made under his directorship (1802–25). Most of the figures are unmarked, and many of the table-wares too. But on the latter a scratched sign resembling a cursive 'N' appears so commonly that it can hardly be dismissed as a turner's mark, and may stand for 'Nove'.

Two plates and a teapot in the Sèvres Museum were almost certainly among the samples produced by Pasquale Antonibon when the factory first became active in 1762. On one plate is Hercules and Nessus; on the other a subject of vases, plates and cups being offered to *La Serenissima* by a maiden symbolizing Le Nove, supported by Time

---

[1] A Venetian who entered Cozzi's factory in Venice at the age of ten, about 1765, and worked for three years at the Vienna factory, whence he was called in 1786 to become director of modellers for Parolin. He died in 1821.

(|) *Plate* 38.

and the city of Bassano (1). The teapot is globular and almost gives the impression of being a Vezzi piece, such as Plate 7A, redecorated by Antonibon; the glaze of the base has been scrubbed off, perhaps removing a previous mark for which 'Nove, Antonio Bon' has been substituted in purple enamel.[1] The sides of the teapot are covered with broad flower-painting, and a label painted in eggy yellow under the spout has the monogram 'GAB' which also appears on the plates. In all these pieces the coloured enamels and sketchy painting look experimental.

The *Giornale d'Italia* in 1765 had notices of Antonibon's porcelain which included 'superb teapots in low relief of masterly execution'. The charmingly fussy example in Plate 30A must be one of them; it is marked 'Nove' twice in raised letters. There exist coffee-pots and sugar basins with similar rococo handles and reliefs. Other early teapots and jugs have gadroons in relief round the bottom, and twig handles. Slight landscape-drawing like that on the teapot, in emerald green, black and crimson, is found also on cups and saucers, as are very sketchy, broad drawings of peasants in landscape with animals. The inkwell in Plate 28B, decorated partly in relief and partly in flat painting, again belongs to the period of Antonibon's own management (1762–73); it carries with it the large vase in Plate 29. The Le Nove factory was economical in its use of moulds—all the applied figures of little boys are from the same model with slight differences in the assembly of limbs (note the loincloth). The same figures were applied as handles to vessels painted in the style of a much later date (2).

Between 1773-81 the porcelain factory must have remained idle. Under Parolin's management (1781–1802) the rococo style apparently remained in favour, and ideas for shapes of useful wares were borrowed from Cozzi at Venice. A bowl and stand with rococo handles, in the Victoria and Albert Museum, is painted with fruit so like that on Cozzi porcelain that only the gilt mark 'Nove' betrays its origin.[2] In the Bassano Museum is a star-marked tea service with twig handles (as Plate 17A) and a version of the Meissen 'onion pattern' painted in green and gold with black outlines. But some smoother, typical neo-classical shapes were soon to appear (3). A peculiarity of the tea and coffee-pots is a pair of holes in the edge of the covers, presumably to hold a chain for attachment to the handle. The fan-shaped jardinière made in two pieces was invented at Vin-

---

[1] Illustrated by E. Hannover, *Pottery and Porcelain*, III, 1925, p. 365, Fig. 575.

[2] A similar covered bowl and stand, painted with incidents in the courtship of an Italian officer, is illustrated by Folnesics in *Kunst und Kunsthandwerk*, XVI, 1913, p. 64. The excellent painting is in the style of about 1800–10.

---

(1) *Plate* 28A; (2) *Plate* 33; (3) *Plate* 34A.

cennes, and may thence have been introduced at Le Nove in its early days by Jean-Pierre Varion. It was much used in Antonibon's maiolica-factory; but the earliest examples in porcelain appear to date from the Parolin period, and the finest are after 1800 (1). Giovanni Marcon has hidden his signature in the landscape on the covered bowl and stand at Bassano (2), and written it in full on the base of the fine jardinière in the Victoria and Albert Museum (3). Three other pieces here illustrated may be his work (4). His line has not the precision of painting found on early Meissen porcelain, but in a sketchy manner he is able to convey a sense of spaciousness most unusual in such a medium. Vast buildings spread into the distance behind the groups of Orientals in a harbour scene or a landscape; the sturdy country girls proffer their robust charms in a setting of romance. Sometimes they are visited by gentlemen wearing top-hats—a coach is seen disappearing round the corner on the saucer in Plate 35B. Marcon's colour-schemes have a peculiar attraction. A soft grey-green contrasts with the emerald in the foliage of trees, and a transparent rose-pink offsets the iron-red in the dresses worn by the figures. The painter had the reputation of an eccentric and is said to have worked only on Tuesdays.

The country idylls, harbour-scenes, and illustrations to Dante painted on Le Nove porcelain were evidently suggested by the popular engravings that issued in great numbers from the famous Remondini press at Bassano. But subjects less congenial to the independent culture of this delightful hillside town were called for after 1796, when Napoleon defeated the Austrians in a bloody battle near Le Nove itself. There is record of cups sent to Venice in 1798, painted with figures of Austrian soldiers in gilt medallions, and marching armies appear in the background of the classical scenes on the covered bowl, Plate 33. It is scarcely necessary to add that such elaborately decorated pieces are rare in comparison with the numerous cups and saucers with *chinoiseries*, swags etc., in a style similar to that of Cozzi's Venetian porcelain.

The passing of the directorship from Parolin to Baroni in 1802 brought no innovations beyond the change to the Empire style, which had already begun. But Baroni made in cream-coloured earthenware some very large and imposing urn-shaped vases with architectural mouldings and handles in the form of female busts. They were usually painted with Homeric or mythological scenes taken from engravings by Edelink after the French seventeenth-century painter Le Brun. A vase in porcelain, somewhat similar in shape, is marked in the

---

(1) *Plate* 30B, 31; (2) *Plates* 32; (3) *Plate* 31; (4) *Plates* 30B, 33, 34C.

painting 'G.B.Nove', and is decorated with the harbour-scenes that remained popular till the end (1).

Le Nove has remained an important centre of the ceramic industry till the present day, making white and cream-coloured earthenware of the Staffordshire type. There are figures and groups in this material obviously related in style to those of porcelain. According to information given to Lady Charlotte Schreiber and published by Chaffers, the Antonibon family attempted to maintain the manufacture of porcelain against an apathetic market until 1835. Some cups and saucers of disagreeably thin 'eggshell' porcelain, painted with *chinoiseries* and marked with a gold star, have been claimed for Le Nove. But their mark with its solid centre, and the presence of examples in the Ginori family collection, support their attribution to the Doccia factory. (See p. 37.)

Porcelain figures were among the products of Le Nove mentioned by the *Giornale d'Italia* in 1765, and the rococo reliefs on the vase with figures in Plate 29 suggest that it is an early piece. Other figures of the Antonibon period (1762–73) are hard to identify, and those illustrated here probably date from after 1781. The stock infants from the vase in Plate 29 reappear on the left of the group in Plate 36A and on the reverse of that in Plate 36B. A family resemblance between all the *contadini* on Plates 36 and 37 is unmistakable; the boys have bullet heads, crisp outstanding curls, and sharp noses continuing the line of the low brow; the short-legged girls smirk vivaciously, and their thick, sturdy bodies impose on their corsets a pressure that can be well appreciated when these are removed (2). Incised inside the rockwork base of the group in Plate 37A is the mark 'Nove', confirming the attribution of the whole series. They may be the work of Domenico Bosello, in the Parolin period. His actual signature is only found on a portrait bust of the *curato* of Le Nove dated 1789,[1] and this is hardly comparable; but a large composite group of Prudence, Fortitude and Humility in the Bassano Museum is held to be Bosello's work of 1810.[2] Certainly by the same modeller is the fine symbolic figure of Venice in Plate 39. Equally solid female figures in the Bassano Museum wear classical undress and are shown making offerings to terminal busts of Mercury and Pan. The treatment of the bases of the Le Nove groups is distinctive. There are holes pierced through the rockwork, partially filled with inserted flowers or tufts of 'moss', and in places the edges

[1] Illustrated by C. Baroni, *Le ceramiche di Nove di Bassano*, p. 69 and Plate X; also by N. Barbantini, *Le porcellane di Venezia e delle Nove*, 1936, Fig. 277. Also Le Nove are Barbantini's Figs. 137, 145–8, 153, 155 (classified by him as Cozzi).

[2] Barbantini, op. cit., Fig. 281. The component figures are also found separately.

(1) *Plate* 35; (2) *Plate* 36A.

of the rocks have been scooped over with a blunt tool. The figures and groups were mostly intended to stand on separate circular pedestals of the kind also made by Cozzi in Venice.

A coloured group of a European merchant and his wares surrounded by Orientals has scratched or painted on his baggage the date 1789, 'Nove', and 'Wenezia' (1); it recalls the scenes painted on useful wares by Marcon. Other figures of men and women in fashionable dress of the late eighteenth century stand, often in pairs, on bases that claim them for Le Nove. The Fitzwilliam Museum, Cambridge, has a large marked group of Hercules and Cerberus; and a grandiose white group of Jupiter defeating the Titans, in the Victoria and Albert Museum, is shown also to be Le Nove by the modelling and material (it has hitherto been wrongly classified and published as Naples).[1] An equally ambitious Deposition from the Cross, with St. Mary Magdalene, St. John and the Instruments of the Passion and stock Le Nove cherubs, has been published by Professor Barbantini.[2]

ESTE (FROM 1781)

Three minor factories at Este concerned themselves with porcelain. G. B. Brunello, who left the Le Nove factory in 1765, attempted with fellow fugitives and stolen materials to make porcelain of his own. He was apparently unsuccessful, and received no official encouragement from the Venetian Board of Trade. We are not concerned with his manufacture of *terraglia* (cream-coloured earthenware), which was continued by his son Domenico.

Jean-Pierre Varion has already been mentioned as a worker at Le Nove.[3] He was probably the Varion named, without initials, as a modeller (*sculpteur*) in the French factory of Vincennes between 1749–52.[4] At Le Nove from 1753, he married after 1756 Fiorina Fabris, daughter of one of Antonibon's workmen, and in the lawsuit of 1765 was said to have deserted Antonibon and gone to Bologna. His attempts to start a porcelain factory there and at Modena in 1776 failed. In 1778 he arrived in Este, and entered into partnership with one Gerolamo Franchini, a goldsmith who had experience of modelling in clay. Both were interested in developing *terraglia* but soon decided

[1] Morazzoni, *Le porcellane italiane*, Plate CV, c.

[2] Barbantini, op. cit., Fig. 153. The other Deposition, Fig. 147, is also Le Nove; an example in Hamburg is illustrated by E. Hannover, *Pottery and Porcelain*, III, 1925, Fig. 566.

[3] See p. 20.

[4] G. Lechevallier-Chevignard, *La manufacture de porcelaine de Sèvres*, 1908, p. 151. Mlle. Marcelle Brunet, Librarian at the Sèvres National Factory, has kindly verified this entry in the Archives as the only reference to Varion.

(1) *Plate* 38.

to work separately. Varion apparently discovered a suitable formula for porcelain; but he died late in 1780, and it was left to his widow Fiorina Fabris to carry on his enterprise. She engaged as her partner Antonio Costa, a former Le Nove workman; and according to documents published by Urbani de Gheltof, in 1781 she obtained from the Venetian Senate two concessions.[1] One gave exemption from customs-duty for materials to make *terraglia*; the other was a privilege by which her firm shared with Cozzi of Venice and Antonibon of Le Nove exclusive rights to manufacture porcelain in Venetia. Franchini seems to have made no porcelain either before or after parting with Varion; but in 1782 he obtained the same concession for *terraglia* as had Fiorina Fabris in the preceding year; and in May 1785 he was granted exclusive rights to make *terraglia* in Este. Fiorina Fabris and Antonio Costa are believed to have continued making porcelain until late in the eighteenth century.

None of their useful wares has been identified except a small unpainted cup without a handle in the Sèvres Museum. It is of hard, translucent yellowish porcelain with the incised mark 'este C.F' (? Costa-Fabris). Of the same material are large figures of the Virgin and St. John from a Crucifixion group, formerly in Lady Charlotte Schreiber's collection and now in the Victoria and Albert Museum (1). On the back of their bases are the incised inscriptions 'ESTE' and 'ESTE. 1783'. The pedestals were made separately and attached with cement. These marked figures now make possible the identification of other figures and groups in the same material and in a similar style— undoubtedly that of Jean-Pierre Varion, who made the original moulds. There are exquisitely designed miniature groups at Turin and in the Victoria and Albert Museum, representing Venus at the forge of Vulcan and Venus appearing to Aeneas and Achates (2). They should stand on bases made separately. In spite of their small scale they show the same firmness of modelling as the figures of the Virgin and St. John, and the same expressiveness of gesture. The lips of Vulcan and Achates are parted in surprise at the apparition of the goddess above them. There is a curious resemblance between these groups and certain engravings in the Paris 1767–71 edition of the Abbé Banier's *Les métamorphoses d'Ovide*—a book which was used by painters at the Doccia factory.[1] The engravings are those by C. Monnet, an artist with a very individual style; one is tempted to think that Varion possessed some illustrations by him for an Aeneid. The group in Plate 42A, adapted from an engraving by A. Legrand or

[1] See p. 37.

(1) *Plate* 40; (2) *Plate* 41.

Pierre Aveline after Boucher entitled *Flore et l'Amour*, can also be identified as Este porcelain by its material, style, and the form of the flowers attached to the base, which appear also on the base of an Aeneid group in the Victoria and Albert Museum. There are modified versions of the Flora and Cupid group in the Fitzwilliam Museum, Cambridge, and in Berlin.[1]

Varion is traditionally remembered as the modeller of a large group of thirty figures representing the assembly on Mount Parnassus. The original was seen by Urbani de Gheltof before 1876 and again in more recent times, but has apparently again disappeared. It is possible that the group in Plate 42B is a re-combination of four figures from the Parnassus—two Muses, an Athenian philosopher with a book and an owl (perhaps Aristotle), and at the back a bearded soldier in Roman dress (perhaps Marcus Aurelius). Separate figures of a Muse and of Aristotle have been seen in biscuit porcelain.

It is sad that an artist of such sensitive gifts as Varion should not have settled earlier at a factory where he could develop them. He was still remembered at Le Nove in 1798, when the bills of the factory included 'figures in the Varion manner', sold at a low price and therefore probably miniatures. It seems likely that the reference was not to early work done by the artist at Le Nove, but to imitations of the figures made by his widow at Este.

TREVISO
and other minor factories

At TREVISO, about 16 miles north of Venice, one G. B. Antonio Rossi and his successor Giovan Maria Roberti appear from the Venetian state documents to have made porcelain between 1759 and 1777, but it has not been identified. Just before the end of the eighteenth century the brothers Andrea and Giuseppe Fontebasso added porcelain to their other ceramic productions, and continued making it till about 1840. A covered bowl of simple shape, in the British Museum, is marked 'FF Treviso 1799' in gold, and has very poor oval landscape panels set in a dark blue ground. Cylindrical cups in the Victoria and Albert Museum and elsewhere bear marks 'GAFF' (Giuseppe Andrea Fratelli Fontebasso) with or without the name of the place; some are also signed by the painter Gaetano Negrisole, with dates between 1830-4. The subjects of the painting include ladies and gentlemen in early nineteenth-century dress, Austrian soldiers, and illustrations to the Idylls of the Swiss poet Salomon Gessner, then recently translated into Italian. The porcelain

[1] Illustrated as Buen Retiro by E. Hannover, *Pottery and Porcelain*, III, p. 383, Fig. 606.

resembles that made by Cozzi in Venice but is greyer in colour and very poorly painted.

At VICENZA, 41 miles west of Venice, the Conte Carlo Vicentini Dal Giglio is said to have made porcelain resembling that of Le Nove between 1793 and 1800. Between 1777–80 porcelain was also made in ANGARANO, a suburb of Bassano, by the widow Ippolita Meneghini-Marinoni, with the help of workmen from Antonibon's porcelain-factory at Le Nove, which was closed at that time. The wares made at these minor factories cannot now be distinguished from those of Le Nove.

4

VINOVO (1776–1820) AND OTHER NORTH-WESTERN FACTORIES

In North-West Italy TURIN had long been the capital of the Dukes of Savoy, who became also Kings of Sardinia after 1720. A maiolica factory founded here in 1725 was about 1736 taken over by Giorgio Giacinto Rossetti. He is thought to have worked previously as a faïence-painter in Marseilles, and was certainly at Lodi near Milan in 1729, when he signed pieces painted in the French *style Berain* popular in Marseilles and Moustiers. In 1737 Rossetti received subsidies from King Carlo Emmanuele to make porcelain, and in 1742 he apparently attracted from Vienna to Turin the porcelain-painter Jacobus Helchis and the otherwise unknown porcelain-artist Anton Wagner. In 1743 he was able to offer samples of porcelain teapots, cups, and ornamental vases. But the manufacture apparently soon ceased, and the only existing pieces so far identified are two small busts of greyish hard-paste porcelain in the Museo Civico at Turin, marked with the cross of Savoy and 'GR' in monogram incised, and with 'TORINO' in underglaze blue.[1]

At VISCHE in Piedmont the Conte Francesco Lodovico Birago de Vische formed in 1765 a Company to make porcelain for twenty years. But he soon disagreed with his associates, and though some porcelain was made in 1766, the factory then failed. In the Museo Civico at Turin are two eye-baths and a small cup with blue ground, bearing the factory-mark of a trefoil and 'W' impressed.

Greater success eventually attended a third factory set up under royal patronage in 1776, in the old fourteenth-century castle of VINOVO six miles from Turin. It was founded by a former associate of the Vische concern, the broker Giovanni Vittorio Brodel. He invited to Turin Pierre-Antoine Hannong, the black sheep of the family who had created the famous faïence-factory at Strasburg (which also made hard-paste porcelain from 1752–5, when that branch of the factory was transferred to Frankenthal in the Palatinate).

[1] V. Viale: '*Porcellane della fabbrica Rossetti di Torino*', in *Faenza*, XXXIV, 1948, p. 118.

Hannong thus had good technical knowledge, but his defects of character became evident during his brief directorship at Strasburg (1760–2), his subsequent attempts to sell the 'secret' of hard-paste porcelain to Sèvres, and his ill-fated ventures in making porcelain on his own at Vincennes and in Paris. In 1778 Brodel retired, and Hannong managed so ill that two years later the factory closed and was sold. But work soon began again under the directorship of a scholarly chemist, Dr. Vittorio Amedeo Gioanetti, who carried it on from 1780 until 1796, when the French invasion caused an intermission of eighteen years. Shortly before his death in 1815 Gioanetti reopened the factory, which lasted under his successor Giovanni Lomello until 1820.

The factory mark was the simple cross of Savoy, usually over the letter 'V', painted in underglaze blue or incised. It was sometimes accompanied by the initials 'D.G.' (Dottore Gioanetti), 'L' (Lomello), or 'CA', a painter's mark.

The paste is of a pleasant creamy tone, and with its glassy glaze looks like soft-paste porcelain. It is actually a hard-paste containing high proportions of magnesite and quartz, and was highly praised by Brongniart, the famous Director of Sèvres in the first half of the nineteenth century.

Lists of stock drawn up when the factory was failing in 1779 have been published by Vignola,[1] and show that figures and groups were already being made besides tea-services, inkstands, covered bowls and knife-handles. From the rich collection in the Museo Civico at Turin it is very evident that Pierre-Antoine Hannong had given a thoroughly French stamp to the whole work of the factory. This can be seen in the shape of the tall teapots (1), of the jugs with cylindrical necks, and of the lobed dishes and plates. There are surviving traces of rococo in the scrollwork of some of the handles, and a tureen dated 1778 with scroll feet has on its cover vegetables in the round, as at Strasburg and Niderviller.[2] But the shapes generally are simple and in good taste, though not very exciting. A characteristic small egg-shaped vase on a spreading foot, with goat's head handles, is already mentioned in 1779.

The decorations include bunches of roses in Strasburg style, using the same 'purple of Cassius' crimson; landscape vignettes in purple or overglaze blue, or in black under transparent green enamel; medallions containing portraits, cupids or landscapes; and the floral swags,

[1] G. Vignola, *Sulle maioliche e porcellane del Piemonte*, 1878, pp. 34–6.
[2] V. Viale, *I Musei Civivi nel 1932*, p. 5, Figs. 7, 8.

(1) *Plate* 43B.

Greek fret, and cornflower patterns common in French porcelain of the late eighteenth century. A distinctive service is painted in gold alone with the arms of Savoy, and a teapot with a portrait of King Vittorio Amedeo is signed by the painter Carpano.

A 'figure representing Minerva with pedestal' (1) was mentioned in 1779, and bears a very close resemblance to the figures modelled by J. W. Lanz at Strasburg and Frankenthal. 'Various painted stags' and 'a dog with a chain' recall the Strasburg animals, and there are reproductions of the graceful models created by Paul-Louis Cyfflé in Eastern France, such as the boy sweep, and the the boy and girl gardeners. There are also some plump children painted in rather strong colours, including bright blue and yellow, that might easily pass as French. The bases are either square, or irregular and painted to represent grass. Some busts of Roman Emperors, medallion portraits of the Savoy family, and goddesses in classical dress are of white glazed or unglazed porcelain, and may be the work of the chief modeller Carlo Tamietti, who gained a high reputation during his employment from 1776 until his death in 1796.

The potter and painter Jacopo Boselli (alias Borelli or Jacques Borelly) is a problematic character who apparently made faïence in Marseilles before setting up in GENOA. Morazzoni quotes references for his work in Genoa between 1779 and his death in 1808; he is said to have made biscuit and other porcelain, but the evidence for this is unsatisfactory. His signature is quite often found on faïence somewhat garishly painted with flowers in enamel colours, and on useful wares of cream-coloured earthenware painted in red.

---

(1) *Plate* 43B.

5

DOCCIA

(1735—*Present Day*)

The powerful state of Tuscany built up by Cosimo I de Medici was in full decline when his last descendant Gian Gastone died in 1737. The Grand Duchy now passed by treaty to Francis III of Lorraine, who, as husband of Maria Theresa, eventually became Emperor of Austria.

The Marchese Carlo Ginori, unkindly described by a contemporary as '*cabalista di natura e macchiavellista di genio*' headed the deputation to Vienna to express loyalty to the new ruler. Apart from the political aptitude which won him the Governorship of Leghorn, Ginori exerted an enlightened curiosity and enterprise worthy of a better age. He reclaimed for agriculture the marshes of Cecina on the Tuscan coast; imported and bred Angora goats for their wool; and introduced goldfish from China to the Austrian court. But his favourite creation was the porcelain factory at Doccia near Florence, which remained under the paternal control of the Ginori family until 1896. From then till the present time it has been incorporated with the Società Ceramica Richard of Milan under the name of Richard-Ginori.

Until the Second World War a museum attached to the factory housed the original wax and plaster models, as well as finished examples of 'old Ginori' porcelain. These belong to the family, and have since been removed elsewhere to storage. Among the models are reduced copies of famous antique statues in Florence and Rome; copies after Michelangelo and Pietro Tacca; and designs, some of which may have been specially commissioned, by Massimiliano Soldani-Benzi (1658–1740) and other contemporary sculptors working in the dramatic baroque tradition established by Bernini in the previous century. Carlo Ginori evidently shared with Augustus the Strong of Saxony an ambition to make large-scale porcelain sculpture, and this so far prevailed over the intractability of the paste as to give to almost all serious figure-work later produced at Doccia a characteristic baroque or academic stamp.

The many pamphlets issued by the factory since 1861 give only a slender and unreliable account of its early history. Morazzoni, following Marryat, was forced to draw much on the evidence of travellers who visited Doccia in the eighteenth and early nineteenth centuries. It appeared that the early archives had been lost. But quite recently they have been discovered among other family papers by the Marchese Leonardo Ginori-Lisci, who is now engaged in the formidable task of editing them for publication. It is through his kindness that some particulars drawn from this work in progress are referred to here. Of special value are the inventories, drawn up on the death of Carlo Ginori in 1757, of stock then held at Doccia and at a showroom in Leghorn.

Experiments with Italian clays apparently began in 1735. While at Vienna in 1737 Carlo Ginori engaged Johann Carl Wendelin Anreiter von Zirnfeld, who is known to have been a *Hausmaler* or independant decorator of porcelain, and may also have worked in the Du Paquier factory. The surviving contract shows that in Florence he was to work as chief painter only—not as an 'arcanist' with knowledge of porcelain paste, as has hitherto been supposed. Anreiter's son Anton, a boy then less than twelve years old, accompanied him to Doccia and later worked there as a painter. Gaspare Bruschi was chief modeller till 1778, assisted towards the end by his son Guiseppe. Carlo Ginori himself seems to have directed the experiments to obtain a satisfactory paste. By 1740 enough progress had been made for him to send Anreiter to Vienna with sample cups, which were shown at Court and favourably compared with those of the Du Paquier and Meissen factories. Ginori obtained forthwith a privilege for making porcelain in Tuscany, but (according to Morazzoni) sales did not begin till 1746. In August of that year both the Anreiters returned to Vienna, where in 1747 Carl Wendelin died and Anton entered the Imperial porcelain factory as a painter. Salmon, author of the *Universal Traveller*, visited Doccia about 1750 and saw a variety of table-wares with decoration in relief and painting; he doubted whether the factory would succeed. Indeed under Carlo Ginori (d. 1757) it probably ran at a financial loss, but the experience gained was invaluable for the future. Lorenzo I Ginori (d. 1791) was able to increase the staff and production, despite the abortive attempt of his brothers to start a rival factory at San Donato.

The factory-mark of a star, taken from the Ginori arms, apparently came into use only towards the end of the eighteenth century. It is found in various colours, and has a more solid centre than the star used at Le Nove, except when it appears in the form of crossed triangles. GINORI, GIN, or GI impressed, are mid-nineteenth marks, as is the crowned 'N' sometimes found on the so-called 'Capodimonte reproductions'.

It is fairly easy to identify most Doccia porcelain by the material.

The so-called *masso bastardo* used from the beginning is a hybrid hard paste, more distinctly grey than any other Italian porcelain. It readily develops 'fire-cracks', and appears to 'drag'; the marks of turning are often visible on shaped vessels, and the porcelain looks and feels rough. The glaze lacks brilliance, has a sticky, smeared appearance, and on early pieces often shows a pronounced green or yellow tinge. (The glaze on Le Nove and on Cozzi's Venetian porcelain is more glassy and brilliant.) From about 1770–90 the Doccia glaze was often made opaque and dead white, probably by an admixture of tin-oxide. A finer and more translucent cold white paste was adopted towards the end of the eighteenth century for wares of the best quality.

The earliest useful wares (1), made under Carlo Ginori between 1740–57, include baroque-style coffee-pots and teapots with snake-like spouts, heavy handles, and domed covers; handle-less tall cups and saucers; and plates or dishes with deeply moulded wavy edges (called *alla francese*, or 'French style' in the records). There are some curious vessels with double walls (2), the outer ones pierced and decorated in relief—an idea borrowed from certain bowls of Fukien *blanc-de-chine* porcelain; the Doccia bowls with pierced walls and applied rams' heads are referred to in the documents as *veggini* or hand-warmers to contain burning charcoal. Pierced cups are recorded, but apparently none survive. To judge from the 1757 inventories, much early useful ware was decorated in underglaze blue. Rare surviving examples show flowering plants oddly painted in greyish blue with the aid of stencils—a practice unique in European eighteenth-century porcelain (3). Hatched shading is used for the playing children on a teapot, and for the naturalistic flowers on a dish here illustrated (4); both the designs and the brushwork suggest Anreiter's familiarity with Du Paquier's Vienna porcelain. The cover of the teapot already shows the clumsy, angular 'lathe-turned' profile that haunts many later Doccia shapes.

A tall handle-less cup in the British Museum is painted in red enamel with the Feeding of the Five Thousand, and signed in minute characters under the base *'Karlo Wendelin Anreiter di Ziernfeldt: Fierenze'*.[1] It is of Chinese (Fukien) porcelain, and must have been painted at Doccia, either as a proof of skill or as a pattern, before success was achieved with the local paste. An almost identical unsigned Doccia cup is in the Ginori family collection, and the 1757

---

[1] Illustrated in M. Jourdain and R. Soame Jenyns, *Chinese export art in the 18th century*, London, 1950, Fig. 107; and by W. B. Honey in *Antiques*, March 1932, p. 126.

---

(1) *Plates* 44–9; (2) *Plate* 44B; (3) *Plates* 44A, 45A (cover); (4) *Plate* 45A, B.

inventory refers to three cups 'painted in red with sacred subjects and an infinity of figures'. Two other lobed cups signed *Carlo Anreiter VZ-Fierenze* have been published as primitive Doccia porcelain,[1] and may well be the samples taken to Vienna in 1740; they have elaborate trellis-work alternating with market-scenes in gold and coloured enamels outside, and solid gilt inside. There is similar gilding on the cup and saucer shown in Plate 46A, which have a polychrome armorial and iron-red monochrome landscapes with very northern-looking buildings. (Anreiter had painted just such landscapes before he came to Florence, on a breakfast set of mixed Meissen and Du Paquier porcelain.)[2] Two fluted oval fruit-dishes in the Ginori family collection, painted with plants and reptiles, bear the signature in fired enamel '*Ant. Anreiter di Zirnfeldt fecit Florentia* 1746',[3] and this may justify the traditional ascription to the younger Anreiter of a series of oval dishes, minutely painted in coloured enamels and tooled gilding, with male and female figures in sixteenth-century oriental dress (1). The flesh-tones are finely stippled in brownish red; the dress, painted in fine hair-strokes, shows a clash between fiery iron-red and violet, and the long-stemmed naturalistic flowers in the border have leaves painted in a sharp transparent emerald green with black outlines. This colour-scheme is characteristic of early Doccia. The flowers, reminiscent of the *deutsche Blumen* on Du Paquier's Vienna porcelain, recur on a coffee-pot and covered bowl (2). But these must be dated after the Anreiters' return to Vienna in 1746. For the Cardinal's arms on the coffee-pot are those of Giovanni Francesco Stoppani, who was elevated to the purple in 1753 (he became Bishop of Palestrina, 1763–74). And the covered bowl bears the arms and motto of the Hervey family, Earls of Bristol; it was probably made for George William (second Earl, 1751–75) during his stay at Turin as envoy extraordinary between 1755–8. Of about the same date are plates, cups and saucers of a service with unidentified heraldry and rich mantling (3). The baroque scrolled dish with Bacchus and Ariadne (4) is remarkable for its challenging colours and the heavy patches of gilding that appear on the shells in the border and parts of the design. A dish from the same mould at Turin has the long-stemmed natural-

---

[1] E. W. Braun, 'Doccia porcelain of the earliest period', *Burlington Magazine*, XIII, 1908, p. 145.

[2] E. W. Braun, 'Neues über den Wiener Porzellanmaler Karl Wendelin Anreiter und die Frühzeit der Manufaktur,' *Kunst und Kunsthandwerk* XVI, 1913, p. 249. See also F. M. Hoffmann, 'Notizen zu Anreiter', in *Anzeiger des Landesmuseums in Troppau*, II, 1931, p. 222.

[3] Morazzoni, Plate IXA.

---

(1) *Plate* 46B; (2) *Plates* 48, 49A; (3) *Plate* 47A; (4) *Plate* 47B.

istic flowers; and another in Professor Barbantini's collection is painted with spectacular heraldry. The thin smear of glaze on the backs of these dishes has fired to a rusty orange colour.

The directorship of Lorenzo I Ginori (1757–91) saw a rapid improvement in the colour and stability of the paste, and the introduction about 1770 of an opaque white tin-glaze. With gradual modification, the baroque shapes and some painted designs invented under Carlo Ginori long continued in use, and Doccia made less concession than other Italian factories to the current rococo style. Teapots and coffee-pots still have snaky spouts, but the handles become lighter and the covers flatter; peculiar to Doccia covers are the pairs of lugs, which fit through slots in the neck of the vessel and hold them firmly in place. A new type of plate, already introduced before 1757, has skewed ribs and basket-work borders in relief, imitated from the Meissen *neu-osier* pattern (1). Cups now have handles, of characteristic shape; their square-edged foot-rings are deeply undercut, and the walls of the cup are very thick just above the foot (2). Twig-shaped handles and applied leaves, fruit or flowers are common on the lobed tureens and large pot-pourri vases (3), whose covers are cut in openwork. The handles on the covers may take the form of a fruit or vegetable, or of small animal groups, which are also found separately (4). There are some oval dishes of irregular shape with rococo relief mouldings, copied almost exactly from those made in the Imperial Vienna factory. Rococo moulded patterns are also found on snuffboxes with painted figures inside the covers.

Some of the painted designs most popular between 1757 and 1780 can be identified in the 1757 inventories, and may have been introduced even earlier. '*A galletto*' refers to the fighting cockerels, usually painted in red and gold (5). 'Miniatures in the Saxon manner with arabesques in red and gold' must refer to the feathery borders in red, gold and purple which enclose landscapes with Chinese or European figures (6)—a type earlier current at Meissen between 1725–35. Doccia pieces with this pattern are found with and without the tin-glaze, and with figures varying much in style; they have sometimes been incorrectly attributed to the Cozzi factory. There are some excellent *chinoiserie* figures in monochrome tooled gilding; and oriental flowers of the Japanese 'Imari' type, in red, gold and underglaze or enamel blue. The very popular pseudo-oriental design now called '*à tulipano*' (7) does not appear under that name in the documents, though it had a very long life. Bunches of European flowers in

(1) *Plate* 50A; (2) *Plate* 49B, C; (3) *Plate* 51B; (4) *Plate* 63A; (5) *Plate* 49B; (6) *Plate* 50A; (7) *Colour-Plate* B p. 36, and *Plate* 49C.

B. *Doccia. About* 1760–70. *D.* 9¾ *in.*
Victoria and Albert Museum
(*See p.* 36)

bright enamel colours are most often found on a ground of tin-glaze, though flowers '*à la Sassonia*' were already mentioned in 1757. The big pot-pourri vase in Plate 51B has an opaque lemon-yellow ground with inset panels of monochrome crimson, through which details are scratched with a sharp point.

Between 1780 and 1800 the same technique of scratching details in white through the colour was used for the foliage of feathery trees, which appear in vignette landscapes, with human figures, buildings and birds (1). As elsewhere, the neo-classical style prescribed some new and simpler shapes, and slightly-painted borders among which a band of dotted circles is typical (2). But on a plate here illustrated (3) the *gros-bleu* border with gilt marbling is a belated adaptation from Sèvres porcelain; the figures of Mercury and Herse are copied from an engraving after H. Gravelot in the Abbé Banier's *Les métamorphoses d'Ovide* (Paris, 1767–71). The same book provided subjects for the exceptionally well-painted covered bowl and stand shown in Plate 51A, whose milder colour-scheme of cold sepia, strong pink, warm blue and blackish green is typical of figures as well as table-wares made after 1780. The signatures in gold 'GBF 1783' on the bowl, and 'F1782' on the stand are those of Giovanni Battista Fanciullacci, who was employed at the factory as a 'miniaturist'. Services with violet cameos and stippled cupids also show excellent painting (4).

After the Napoleonic invasion of Italy a cold white translucent paste was introduced at Doccia, possibly containing kaolin imported from Saint-Yrieix near Limoges. From 1792 to 1815 wares of the finest quality are said to have been marked with an incised 'F' (5); second-best with 'PS', and ordinary ware with the star. In the first quarter of the nineteenth century Doccia followed with exceptional competence the almost universal European fashion of painting coldly realistic views, animals, fruit and flowers. There is also a distinct class of tall cups with simple handles and saucers, made in an extremely thin white 'eggshell' porcelain, and marked with a six-pointed star in gold (examples in the Victoria and Albert Museum and the Ginori Collection). They are painted in colours with *chinoiserie* figures in the manner of the engraver Pillement, or with Chinese rocks and flowers in a thick upstanding blue outlined in gold. They have sometimes been attributed to Le Nove, but were almost certainly made at Doccia between 1830 and 1850.

Before discussing figures in the round, it will be convenient to mention figure-subjects in relief. The large white plaque in Plate 56,

---

(1) *Plates* 52A, 53; (2) *Plate* 53A; (3) *Plate* 52A; (4) *Plate* 52B; (5) *Plate* 53B.

a work of great sculptural excellence, is mentioned in one of the early Doccia inventories as 'Time discovering Beauty', by Massimiliano Soldani-Benzi.[1] It is taken from a model made by the sculptor in 1695, for Prince Johann Adam Andreas of Liechtenstein; the bronze version then cast from it is in Vienna.[2] Two early Doccia white reliefs with mythological subjects, in the Museo della Floridiana at Naples, show similar sculptural boldness. A framed relief-portrait, richly enamelled and gilt, shows Maria Theresa flatteringly as a woman still young, though it must date from about 1750–5 (1). Somewhat later is part of a very large vase (2), which has almost lost itself under a riot of baroque high-relief decoration of mythological figures with cupids and tritons in attendance.[3] It is painted in strong colours, including the typical opaque lemon-yellow, stippled flesh-tones, and patches of heavy gilding. In the Museo Civico at Turin are two very large white vases in similar style, and the original wax model for one still survives in the Ginori Collection.[4] Yet another vase of this type, in the Marquess of Bristol's collection, has on one side a relief of Neptune revelling, and on the other a crimson-painted landscape similar to that in our Plate 51B.

Conceived in the same sculptural spirit as the large vases are the miniature mythological, religious, and hunting subjects moulded in low relief on useful wares (3). In studying these we must once for all set aside the preconception, which after a hundred years is still firmly entrenched in Italy, that they have something to do with Capodimonte. The type was in fact created by Doccia in the earliest years of the factory. The writer had almost reached this conclusion before finding it abundantly confirmed in the documents recently discovered by Marchese Leonardo Ginori-Lisci. Some of the designs—Venus and Mars in the net,[5] the Gods overthrowing the Giants,[6] Apollo and Marsyas, and the Judgement of Paris—are known in a series of Italian bronze plaquettes dating from the sixteenth century; they are

[1] The subject is actually 'Time discovering Truth'.

[2] E. Tietze-Conrat. 'Die Bronzen der fürstlich Liechtensteinschen Kunstkammer' in *Jahrbuch des Kunsthist. Inst. der K. K. Zentralkommission für Denkmalpflege*, XI, 1917, p. 84, Fig. 66.

[3] The missing neck fitted into a hole left at the top, and the lower part of the rectangular foot has been sawn off. Hitherto the vase has been wrongly ascribed to Capodimonte.

[4] Joseph Marryat rightly recognised the Turin ewers as Doccia in 1868, when they were in private collections in England. (*A history of pottery and porcelain*, 3rd ed., 1868, Fig. 247.) Morazzoni illustrates the wax model in his Plate XXXVIII and attributes it to the sculptor Guiseppe Piamontini.

[5] Morazzoni, *Le porcellane italiane*, Plate LVIII, for the subjects on lead moulds.

[6] Morazzoni, Plate LVI for the subject on a porcelain tureen.

(1) *Plate* 54; (2) *Plate* 57; (3) *Plate* 55A.

now thought to have been invented by Guglielmo della Porta (d. 1577) or some other artist connected with Michelangelo.[1] It has been shown that the designs were often reproduced by decorators of the seventeenth century[2]; and Morazzoni illustrates the eighteenth-century versions in lead that are still preserved in the Ginori family collection. He accepts the story that these lead moulds and the porcelain vessels prepared from them were made at Capodimonte. There is nothing to support this in the archives of the Capodimonte and Royal Neapolitan factories, which were not interested in reproducing Renaissance designs. Contrary to the Neapolitan custom, genuine examples of the porcelain with relief-decoration are invariably unmarked. Their colouring, and the *masso bastardo* material of which they are made, are those of Doccia. And further proof is now available in the Ginori-Lisci Archives. In an undated price-list of about 1755–65 cups in 'white with figure-subjects in low relief (*con bassorilievo istoriati*) and two handles' are relatively expensive; dearest of all are cups 'with figure subjects in low relief like the above, but painted and gilt'. 'Saucers with garlands in relief, painted' must refer to examples such as that in our Plate 55A. Among the subjects on cups in the Victoria and Albert Museum are Bacchus, Ceres, Phoebus and Neptune in their chariots; the Deluge; a standing angel, and a female figure symbolizing Architecture. A fine tureen and stand in the Palace at Capodimonte has the Gods and Giants.[3] These wares seem not to be found with a tin-glaze, and their colouring suggests a date before 1780.

How did the misconception arise that these wares were made at Capodimonte? 'About ten years ago,' wrote Marryat in 1857, 'a dealer of Leghorn used to order once a year a set of embossed teacups resembling the Capo di Monte, which he procured at La Doccia at two dollars each, and, in the course of the bathing season, managed to dispose of as genuine for about twelve. Upon this discovery, the manufactory began to make this ware extensively upon its own account, and it became a most profitable trade.'[4] Marryat ascertained from a workman at Doccia aged 86 that the moulds had been used there as long as he could remember, which would take them well back into the eighteenth century. As they were not mentioned in such records as he could find at Doccia, Marryat conjectured that Marchese Lorenzo I

[1] L. Planiscig, *Kunsthistorisches Museum in Wien: Die Estensische Kunstsammlung*, 1919, Nos. 395–410. Other examples in the Victoria and Albert Museum.
[2] E. Tietze-Konrat. 'Die Erfindung in Relief: ein Beitrag zur Geschichte der Kleinkunst', *Jahrbuch der Kunsthistorischen Sammlungen in Wien*, XXXV, 1920, pp. 156–7.
[3] Morazzoni, *Le porcellane italiane*, Plate LVI.
[4] Joseph Marryat, *A history of pottery and porcelain*, 2nd ed., 1857, p. 332; see also 3rd ed. 1868, pp. 469, 471.

Ginori might have procured them during one of his coral-fishing expeditions to the Bay of Naples. His conjecture has been improved on by later Italian writers, including Morazzoni, who suggests without evidence that the moulds were bought by Marchese Leopoldo Carlo Ginori at the sale of the Neapolitan Royal Factory's effects about 1830. But the whole idea seems to have originated in the mind of the Leghorn dealer, who found that rich and ignorant tourists paid more for objects allegedly made at the royal and defunct factory of Capodimonte than they would for anything made at a factory still in existence. Unhappily the name has stuck, creating great confusion among collectors, museums and writers on ceramics.[1] In 1857 Marryat gently reproached the contemporary Marchese Lorenzo II Ginori for not putting the Ginori factory mark on the so-called 'Capodimonte reproductions'. Perhaps it was after Marryat's third edition in 1868 (where the fact is not mentioned) that the business-like nobleman began adding the crowned 'N' mark of the Royal Naples Factory—a manoeuvre which Morazzoni and his other encomiasts have found embarrassing to explain! (It should, however, be remembered that the respectable Coalport factory in England behaved just as oddly with its reproductions of Sèvres porcelain.) The teapot in Plate 55B bears the crowned 'N' mark impressed, but has a typical Doccia 'revived rococo' handle and cover with lugs for attachment. Fussy gilt handles and spouts, or improbable handles shaped and painted to imitate coral, are found on other mid-nineteenth century coffee-pots and teapots with relief decoration, made in the *masso bastardo* paste. But the simpler pieces are often baffling; poor colours and painting, with thin black outlines, may help to distinguish them from genuine eighteenth century examples, which have carefully stippled flesh-tones and thick, bright gilding.

Related to the useful wares with low-relief decoration is a series of glazed medallions, about $2\frac{7}{10}$ inches in diameter, with inscribed portraits of the Medici family in white relief against a background of underglaze blue. The documents suggest that the moulds were prepared before 1740 by Massimiliano Soldani-Benzi from earlier bronze medallions by himself and other artists. A whole series is applied to a fine *tempietto* at Cortona which dates from 1755.[2] Late in the century Doccia, like other factories, made unglazed cameo portraits in the style of Wedgwood's blue jasper ware.

Doccia figures and groups are mistakenly attributed to Capodimonte,

[1] Morazzoni illustrates twenty-one Doccia pieces as Capodimonte, and nine as Venice (Cozzi). In Eisner de Eisenhof's book on Capodimonte five Doccia items are illustrated, and in E. Hannover's *Pottery and Porcelain*, Vol. III (English edition, 1925), all eight illustrations of Capodimonte actually represent Doccia porcelain.
[2] See p. 43.

but their characteristics at once emerge when many can be seen together, as in the Museo Civico at Turin. We may start with the more
popular and less pretentious models. They have large, clumsy hands;
small heads with receding brow and chin; iron-red stippling for
flesh-tones (especially noticeable on the hands, where the colour often
runs between the fingers, giving an unpleasant 'gory' effect); black
stippling round the eyes, and hair drawn in fine brown or purple-
brown lines. The colours are garish, with purple-crimson, an opaque
lemon-yellow, and opaque pale blue very much in evidence. On
dresses a 'shot' effect is often contrived with red or purple stippling in the shadows grading off to white or pale lemon-yellow in
the high lights. The paste is the typical Doccia *masso bastardo*, with
its uneven sticky glaze, gaping with the most alarming fire-cracks
when the piece is of any size. Where the surface is unglazed under
the solid bases, an orange smear develops owing to the presence of
iron.

Among the earliest of these figures are *Commedia dell'Arte*
characters mounted with cabbage-shaped bowls on bases encrusted all
over with sea-shells (1). (A *rinfrescatoio con Pulcinella*, mentioned in
the 1757 inventories, corresponds with the surviving examples in
size.) Of the same class is a figure of *Amphitrite and attendants* on a
high, rocky base; and classical deities standing in pairs on the edge of
bowls shaped as tridacna-shells.[1] Much more successful are the
smaller figures which usually stand on square marbled bases (2); some
of these have dresses painted in the unmistakable fiery iron-red of
Doccia, and the Comedy figures show a passionate conviction of
gesture which puts them second only to those of Capodimonte among
Italian porcelain. These small Comedy figures are found also in porcelain of the Viennese Imperial Factory, but though there is some doubt
as to priority of invention, the Doccia examples are much superior in
style. Some miniature groups of animals (3), mentioned as *caccine*
(small hunting subjects) in the 1757 inventories, were often applied as
handles to the covers of tureens; there are later coloured versions on
scrolled rococo bases dating from about 1770. The same inventories
quote miniature figures of *pygmies* and *caramogi* (this word appears
to mean grotesque dwarfs). There are many figures of sea-monsters
supporting shell-shaped sweetmeat dishes, in the manner of the
baroque fountains of Rome (4), and recumbent grotesque sphinxes are
found with screw-holes through their backs for use as corner supports
to wooden pedestals. A set of four *Seasons*, with or without attach-

[1] Morazzoni, Plate LXXVIIc.

---

(1) *Plate* 60c; (2) *Plates* 60A, B; 61A; (3) *Plate* 63A; (4) *Plate* 61c.

ments to hold candles, are known from the documents to have been modelled from carved ivory figures by the Bavarian sculptor Balthasar Permoser (1651–1732). The ivories were at that time in Carlo Ginori's possession but are now lost. The Seasons appear on simple bases, and in a later version on scrolled rococo bases painted in crimson, as in the admirable figure of *Ceres (Summer)* illustrated here (1). A fine figure of a *boy holding a cockerel*, with a similar base, is adapted from a Meissen model (2). Twenty-four *oriental figures* are mentioned in a factory list of about 1780—the *Persian lady* in Plate 61B is one of them, and is coated with the opaque tin-glaze. These oriental figures, some of which are found also in Capodimonte, may have been copied from the Meissen models made in the 1740's, but their ultimate source is the illustrations of Count Charles de Ferriol's *Différentes nations du Levant* (Paris, 1714). The archives will doubtless help in ascertaining the date when the various models so far described were first made at Doccia. But it should be remembered that the paste, glaze and colouring are better guides to the date of the actual figures, which may have been produced over a long period.

A factory-list of about 1780 mentions many *pastorelli* and *pastorelle*, and a white group of two *peasants at their outdoor meal* (3), full of humorous detail, comes early in a series which probably continued into the early nineteenth century. The figures are often grouped with a tree on high hollow rockwork bases, strengthened inside with cross-struts. The parallel combed striations on the rocks are an aid to identification, and coloured examples have a good deal of the cold sepia found also on late eighteenth-century useful wares. A group of *Hagar, Ishmael and the Angel* (4) is obviously related to the peasant-groups, but its finer modelling and elevated pathos also link it with the baroque works illustrated in Plates 56–9. Similar in colour and modelling is the group representing the *Triumph of Tuscany* which stands at the top of a pyramidal table-centre in the Victoria and Albert Museum.[1] This may be identical with a table-centre of the same subject, mentioned in an inventory of the factory dated 1799. Otherwise the military trophies and captive Moors which form the second tier of this composition, and the eight sphinxes that support the wooden base, might from their ugly opaque colours be suspect as later additions.

The documents will probably shed new light on relations between Carlo Ginori and Massimiliano Soldani-Benzi. As that excellent

[1] Illustrated by Morazzoni, Plate XLIII, and E. Hannover, *Pottery and porcelain*, III, p. 373, Fig. 592.

(1) *Plate* 62A; (2) *Colour Plate* c; (3) *Plate* 62B· (4) *Plate* 63B.

C. *Doccia. About* 1770. *Ht.* $5\frac{5}{8}$ *in.*
Victoria and Albert Museum
(*See p.* 42)

sculptor died in 1740 at the age of 82, he cannot have had much time or energy to produce new work for the factory. Some of his wax models, acquired by Ginori, had been used much earlier in making bronzes—the plaque shown in Plate 56, and a set of life-size heads of *Roman Emperors* and Empresses. But a *Lamentation over the dead Christ*, still in the Ginori family collection, seems to have been a new model; and a splendid example of this in white porcelain, mounted on an ebony base with attached porcelain cherubs, swags and supports, is in the Corsini Gallery at Florence. Coloured examples are in the National Museum, Stockholm, and in the collection of the Hispanic Society, New York. The *Pietà* in the British Museum[1] is from a different but similar model (1). The *St. Andrew* in Plate 58, a free adaptation from the great statue set up by Francois Duquesnoy (Il Fiammingo) in 1640 under the Dome of St. Peter's, Rome, is attributed to Gaspare Bruschi, chief modeller at the Doccia factory. It and a companion figure of *St. John* in the Ginori collection are of imposing size, being over three feet high. The same collection includes a great baroque chimneypiece and overmantel with terms and allegorical figures (after Michelangelo) in the round. There is also a life-size bust portrait of Carlo Ginori. In the Palazzo Casali at Cortona is a remarkable baroque *tempietto*, with figures of the Four Continents at the corners, a group of Time bearing off Beauty between the four piers, and other figures at the top; the whole composition, which dates from 1755, is hung with medallion portraits of the Medici family. The Museo Civico at Turin has several very large figures—a *faun carrying a young satyr*, and the *satyr Marsyas bound*, in white porcelain; and another Marsyas and a splendid *Jupiter with his eagle*, painted in typical Doccia colours.

Such works are unlikely to appeal to those who have no sympathy for the baroque in its earnest and grandiloquent Italian form. Yet they are undeniably impressive, both for their sculptural power and for the immense demands they make of the material. At Meissen too it had been hoped that porcelain would serve the ends of serious sculpture; but the material made demands of its own, and through the satiric genius of Kaendler, found its most appropriate expression in the fantastic and artificial grace of table-ornaments. By these standards Doccia might be held to have trespassed beyond the limits proper to porcelain, though it must ever command admiration for its generous aims.

[1] The group formerly belonged to Mr. Gladstone, the Prime Minister, who had a good collection of Italian porcelain.

(1) *Plate* 59.

The rough texture and greyish colour of the *masso bastardo* paste showed up to worse advantage in the large copies of Antique sculpture —the life-size *Flora Farnese* and the *Knife-Grinder* (*Arrotino*), the *Venus de Medici*, *Apollo Belvedere* etc. These were already being made in the time of Carlo Ginori. The figures in unglazed biscuit porcelain attempted later in the eighteenth century are hardly known outside the Ginori family collection. Of the copies after Renaissance sculpture, the Moorish captive in Plate 61D is one of four derived from Pietro Tacca's sculptures on the monument to Grand Duke Ferdinand I of Tuscany at Leghorn, erected between 1623–6.

During the nineteenth century the factory turned out a number of elaborate groups which may have been taken from earlier moulds. These are sometimes mounted on ornate bases with gilding in the 'revived rococo' style which we in England associate with Rockingham and Coalport porcelain. To this class belongs a group in the Cecil Higgins Museum, Bedford, showing Bacchus and Ariadne with a satyr.

As the Doccia factory so competently reproduced its own early models, it is hardly necessary to speak of fakes. But imitations of the pseudo-Capodimonte relief-wares have been made in Paris and Germany (by Ernst Bohne and Sons of Rudolstadt and others), often with a crowned 'N' as a mark. A gold fleur-de-lis (a Capodimonte mark) has been later added to an apparently genuine eighteenth-century Doccia bowl of this class, now in America:[1] and a white saucer in the Victoria and Albert Museum shows traces of an added fleur-de-lis in blue. The bowl and cover in Plate 50B have the Vezzi mark 'Vena' added in un-fired gold paint, and a gold anchor has been similarly added to the piece in Plate 52A.

[1] Illustrated by A. Eisner de Eisenhof, *Le porcellane di Capodimonte*, 1925, Plate 1 (centre); now in Judge Untermyer's Collection, New York.

6

THE BOURBON FACTORIES

Capodimonte (1743–59); *Buen Retiro* (1760–1808);
Naples, Royal Factory (1771–1806).

In 1734 Charles of Bourbon, son of Philip V of Spain by his second marriage to Elisabetta Farnese, became the first king to rule directly over Naples and Sicily since they passed under the Spanish Viceroys in 1502. By eighteenth-century standards he was a benevolent as well as an able ruler. He built the Palaces of Capodimonte and Caserta, and supported the excavations of Herculaneum which began in 1738. But porcelain, next to hunting, became his favourite pastime through his marriage to Maria Amalia Christina of Saxony in that same year. For her father, Augustus II (the Strong) of Saxony and King of Poland, was founder of the Meissen factory, then at the height of its fame, and as part of her dowry she brought no fewer than seventeen porcelain table-services.

After wide search for raw materials Charles opened his own factory in the grounds of Capodimonte (on the northern outskirts of Naples) in 1743. It lasted only sixteen years. For Charles, called in 1759 to succeed his half-brother Ferdinand VI as King of Spain, could not bear to abandon it. Most of the staff and movable equipment went with him, to continue work from 1760 near the Buen Retiro palace in Madrid. This factory lasted till the Peninsular Campaign, when the buildings were fortified by the French (1808), and destroyed by the British (1812).

Charles' eight-year-old son Ferdinand IV remained as King of Naples in 1759. He revived the local manufacture of porcelain in 1771. This 'Royal Factory' flourished till 1806, when Ferdinand took refuge in Palermo from the Napoleonic troops. Under Joseph Bonaparte (1806–8) and Joachim Murat (1808–15) the factory was leased to a French firm, Poulard Prad and Co., who ruined it long before its formal abolition in 1834.

We have, then, to consider the work of three related Bourbon factories. It would simplify matters if collectors and others would recognise Capodimonte and the 'Royal Factory, Naples' as quite distinct. There persists, even in Italy, a belief that many products of

Doccia were made at Capodimonte—thanks to the deliberate mis-representation mentioned on page 39. The Doccia work can be easily identified and dismissed. But to distinguish between the wares made at Capodimonte and some of those made at Buen Retiro is almost impossible; for one factory was the direct continuation of the other, with the same patron, the same staff, and the same factory-mark— the Bourbon fleur-de-lis. For a while the Spanish factory even appears to have used a paste composed of materials imported from Italy. In Northern Europe Capodimonte has long been under a cloud, owing to the suspicion aroused by the Doccia 'reproductions'. It has therefore become customary to attribute all Charles III porcelain to Buen Retiro. To correct this error, and to determine what can most surely be claimed for Capodimonte, is an essential part of this present study.

CAPODIMONTE

About the history, staff, and early productions of the Capodimonte factory much may be learnt from the Neapolitan State Archives, extracts from which have been published by Minieri Riccio and Morazzoni. Unfortunately the documentation for the objects made after 1750 is very slender. It is clear that no secrets about the com-position of the paste were obtained from Meissen, though constant references suggest that examples of Meissen porcelain were available to the artists for imitation. Between 1741–3 unsuccessful attempts were made to lure from Doccia 'the two Germans'[1] working there, and from Vienna the *virtuosi* Anton Wagner and Jacobus Helchis.[2] The composition of the paste was at first entrusted to Livio Ottavio Schepers, who had previously worked in the Neapolitan mint; but he proved dishonest and a trouble-maker, and in 1744 was dismissed in favour of his more ingenious son Gaetano Schepers, whose own recipe gave excellent results for the whole duration of the factory. Giuseppe Gricci was chief modeller throughout. Giovanni Caselli directed the painters till his death in 1752. The Saxon Johann Sigismund Fischer[3] worked as a leading painter from 1754 until he ate a fatal meal of poisonous fungi in 1758. Luigi Restile succeeded him as chief painter, but refused to follow the factory to Spain.

Minieri Riccio quotes very detailed records of progress between 1743 and 1745, when the productions were first put on sale in a series of annual fairs. Snuff-boxes, cane-handles, and tea-services formed the majority; but there were also soup-tureens and large vases with covers

---

[1] The Anreiters. See p. 33.

[2] Wagner is otherwise unknown. Helchis is known as a painter on Du Paquier's Vienna porcelain, and also worked at Turin (p. 29).

[3] Previously at Le Nove (p. 20).

'in the Saxon manner' (*ad uso di Sassonia*). These last were made in 'chimney-piece sets' (*giuochi da camino*) of five, and followed in shape rather than in decoration the well-known Meissen vases bearing the 'A R' monogram of Augustus the Strong (1). Before embarking on figures, the modeller Gricci made moulds for handles and for shell-shaped snuff-boxes, which as early as 1744 had ladies painted inside the cover (2). Gricci must also have modelled the shell-shaped ewers and basins (3). The gem-cutter Ambrogio di Giorgio cut moulds for portrait-medallions, for 'baskets with pierced feet' (possibly to be identified with examples such as Plate 71B, a copy of a Meissen shape); and for 'fruit with the accompanying leaves', probably intended as ornamental attachments to vases and table-wares (4). A 'porcelain tulip' and 'flowers of porcelain' are mentioned in 1745 and 1752, the former made by the modeller Gaetano Fumo. A clock-case was sold in 1747. It is not possible to identify in the published extracts the *blanc-de-chine* (Fukien) porcelain with applied prunus-sprays, which was imitated at Capodimonte as at most other factories at an early stage in their existence (5).

The Archives are so explicit about the painted designs on the earliest useful wares that these can be readily identified in existing examples of perhaps slightly later date. The painter Giuseppe della Torre specialised in tea-services with *battaglie* (battles)[1] (6), *marini* (sea-scapes) (7), *paesi* (landscapes) (8), *istoriati* (figure-subjects), and *amori* (cupids). At first these were painted only in monochrome—blue, violet, black, *paonazzo* (crimson) and red. Figure-subjects with 'arabesques in gold' are already mentioned in 1745, and this class probably included both the garden-parties in contemporary dress and the idyllic scenes of classical nymphs and deities (9). Maria Caselli, niece of Giovanni Caselli, specialised in painting flowers, monochrome and coloured (10). Snuff-boxes and cups painted *alla cinese*, or with 'coloured Chinese flowers' first appear among the productions of 1745–7, and the hesitant painting on the cup shown in Plate 67A suggests that it may be one of the earliest examples of Capodimonte *chinoiserie*. The tall cup in Plate 65B lacks a handle, and is obviously early. Oriental flower-painting of the kind shown in Plate 73A is found in the decorations of the Portici porcelain-room (to be described later), which dates from 1757–9; but this sort of ornament was also

---

[1] A tea-service with battles priced at 450 ducats was the most expensive item in the sales-list of 1745. Was it the actual one here illustrated?

---

(1) *Plates* 68, 69; (2) *Plates* 75A, B; (3) *Plates* 74B, C; (4) *Plate* 70B; (5) *Plate* 74A; (6) *Plates* 66, 67C; (7) *Plate* 67B; (8) *Plates* 64A, B; (9) *Plates* 68, 71A, 72B; (10) *Plates* 69, 70.

much in favour for the ornamental vases made in the early years of Buen Retiro. Minieri Riccio records that in 1746 Caselli was attempting to obtain from Paris five or six dozen engravings 'in the Chinese style, with figures, landscapes and flowers'; but according to a note by Eisner de Eisenhof, the Neapolitan Ambassador in Paris reported that they were not obtainable there, and could be bought at Augsburg or Nuremberg. The characteristic still-life subjects of fruit (1) are not specifically mentioned in Riccio's extracts, but may belong to the category of 'natural objects' (*cose naturali*). On some tea-services the fruit-painting is enclosed by a gold frame of irregular outline, and the rest of the surface covered with a ground of pale turquoise enamel—on which simple tree-patterns are painted in gold. The idea of the turquoise ground certainly derives from Meissen porcelain and not from Vincennes; it is perhaps referred to in the sales-list of 1745 as a 'blue service with thread of gold' (*giuocho turchino con filo di oro*).

As shown by the pieces in Plates 64–71, the Capodimonte material is a beautiful soft-paste 'frit' porcelain, usually pure white, and highly translucent. (It sometimes has a pink or yellow tinge, but is rarely as yellow as Buen Retiro.) The glaze fits closely, is lustrous without being too glassy, and often 'misses' under the foot, where the factory-mark of a fleur-de-lis in underglaze blue is almost invariably present. Sometimes, perhaps deliberately, the glaze is fired to a matt, vellum-like surface which is admirable for painting (2). The material has better plastic qualities than any French soft paste, the cups and saucers being made very thin; but in the larger pieces the walls are thick, and there is at first a cautious simplicity of shape (3). The earliest cups have no handles, and recall in their tall and short shapes the early cups of Meissen and Vienna. When handles appear they seem to be adapted from the kinked Meissen handles of the 1740's (4), and a white cup in the Victoria and Albert Museum actually imitates the relief-designs of the famous Meissen 'Swan Service' made for Count Brühl between 1737–41. The teapot and coffee-pot of a fine service in the same Museum (5) have domed covers and rather clumsily moulded enrichments at spout and handle that resemble shapes current at Meissen between 1725–35. All shapes so far mentioned are quite free from any suggestion of the rococo style; their affinities are with the German late baroque, and it is hard to conceive why they have hitherto been so often classified as Buen Retiro porcelain made after 1760.

We have the Portici porcelain-room to prove the development at

---

(1) *Plate* 65A; (2) *Plate* 68; (3) *Plates* 68, 69, 70A; (4) *Plate* 64A; (5) *Plates* 66, 67C.

Capodimonte in 1757–9 of a thoroughgoing rococo style (1); but this style was also much in favour during the years that immediately followed the transfer of the factory to Spain. In consequence there exists a fairly large category of objects whose attribution between Capodimonte and Buen Retiro is not easy. It is however certain that at Buen Retiro little attention was given to useful wares, and with these the probability lies in favour of Capodimonte. Plates and dishes, with wavy edges and a rim strengthened with heavy mouldings against warping, are often of the finest white paste and painted with all the care one would expect of the older factory (2). Their form was perhaps suggested by those made at Doccia (3). In 1758 King Charles ordered a table service for twenty-four to be made for the Spanish court, and this may perhaps be identified with a series of plates and dishes that still survives in the Museums of Madrid (4). The paintings of gentlefolk and peasants in landscape are in excellent Capodimonte style. There are plates of a different and probably later shape, painted with figures in rather feeble rococo medallions, which might still be Capodimonte (5). Almost certainly from the Italian factory are some ewers with crimson-feathered rococo spouts and handles, somewhat carelessly painted with figures in landscape on the front (6). In the Museo Municipal, Madrid, is a large tureen with a lobster and vegetables in the round on the cover, an asymmetrical moulded cartouche on the side, vine-twig handles, and a channelled and waved surface.[1] It bears the same deeply impressed fleur-de-lis mark as the early Capodimonte figures, and there appears to be no proof that this impressed mark was also used in Spain. Closely related to this tureen in style are vases with channelled surfaces and vine-stem handles, which are also likely to have been made at Capodimonte (7). A large oval wine-cooler in the collection of Doña Maria Bauzá in Madrid again has the impressed mark, channelled waves, and heavy rococo scroll feet and handles.[2] It is of fine white paste and may well be Capodimonte. On the other hand a vessel somewhat similar in style, in the Victoria and Albert Museum, is of inferior yellow paste and should certainly be attributed to Buen Retiro (8).

Certain mannerisms of Capodimonte painting deserve notice. The colours are usually stippled on, or in the case of flowers, drawn in very fine hair lines. Flesh-tones are often shaded in violet; and on poly-

---

[1] Illustrated in Perez-Villamil, *Catalogo . . . colleccion Laiglesia*, Plate XXI, No. 264.
[2] Illustrated by M. Olivar Daydí, *La porcelana en Europa*, II, 1953, Fig. 244. It was illustrated by Marryat when it was in an English collection.

---

(1) *Plate* 81; (2) *Plates* 72B, 73A; (3) *Plate* 47A; (4) *Plate* 72B; (5) *Plate* 73B; (6) *Plate* 72A; (7) *Plate* 75C; (8) *Plate* 88B.

chrome pieces there are almost always clouds in violet and pale orange-red. The colouring generally is soft and harmonious, with a distinctive pale orange red and a good deal of grey-green, olive-green, and brown. The gilt border-patterns are akin to the formal *Laub und Bandelwerk* found on Meissen and early Vienna porcelain—often they bear a surprising resemblance to those on pieces decorated at Augsburg by the *Hausmaler* of the Seuter family. They are, however, simpler than the German work, probably because the Capodimonte artists found the gold difficult to manipulate. It is laid on thick, but is very granular and apt to wear off.

The Neapolitan Archives mention a number of figures and groups modelled by Giuseppe Gricci between 1743–5; a Pantalone, group of two figures, group of three figures, Pulcinella, Madonna della Pietà, St. Sebastian, Immaculate Conception, Bacchus, shepherd with she-goat, *poveri* (poor people), woman spinning, and various animals. This is naturally not a complete list, for many must have been made after 1745, but it indicates that Gricci's range of subjects was wide, and justifies the ascription to him of a series of figures which are among the most attractive in the whole range of European porcelain (1). They show a remarkable grasp of the extremely beautiful but not very plastic material, whose pure whiteness is enhanced by the sparing touches of gold and soft colour on the dresses, and the violet stippling or dabs of pale orange on the cheeks. The modelling is broad, with little detail, and owes its vividness to an unerring grasp of bodily poise and gesture. The big 'Capitano Spacca' at Milan, from the Italian Comedy, is an early piece marred by fire-cracks, with slight and badly fired touches of gilt, black and brownish red[1] (2). The Museo Civico at Turin has a large group of Angelica and Medoro which shows similar defects in paste and the same primitive colours. In the Italian Comedy subjects, the street-hawkers and fishermen (*poveri?*), the young lovers, and the servants playing practical jokes on each other or on their masters, there is a mocking but not cruel humour; over the tiny imbecile faces flit suspicion, meanness, or radiant good cheer. The figures have remarkably small heads. Groups of small punctures in the irregular pad bases imitate moss, and are sometimes touched with green. Marks, when present, are a large fleur-de-lis impressed in a circular hollow, or less commonly painted in underglaze blue. These figures are untouched by the rococo style, and were probably made between 1743 and about 1756.

Plate 78 shows a rather pompous equestrian figure in Roman dress,

[1] Compare the 'Pantalone' modelled in 1744.

(1) *Plates* 76, 77, 79, 80 and *Colour Plate* D; (2) *Plate* 79.

D. *Capodimonte. About 1750. Ht. 8¼ in.*
Cambridge, Fitzwilliam Museum
(See p. 50)

carrying a shield with four gold fleur-de-lis. It is detachable from the horse, which stands on a high baroque base with exceptionally well-painted battle scenes. More closely related to the small figures in mood is the charming Chinese lady who sits on a scrolled rococo base, holding cornucopiae to form a chandelier (1). There are chandeliers like this in the Museo di San Martino at Naples and the Museo Arqueologico Nacional in Madrid. They are closely akin in style to the Portici Porcelain-Room of 1757–9, and the similar room at Aranjuez in Spain (1760–7); in fact they may once have stood in those rooms. Were the moulds taken from Italy to Spain in 1759? The paste is the pure white of Capodimonte, in whichever country they were made.

Gricci's power as a more serious sculptor is seen in a very remarkable large group, about 21 inches high, of the Virgin Mary bending over the dead Christ with a separate figure of St. John standing on the same rocky base. There is a white example in the Villa Floridiana, Naples, and a coloured one in the Museo Municipal, Madrid.[1] This might be the Madonna della Pietà whose model Gricci made in 1744; it is emotionally baroque in feeling; and both the paste and the colouring would suggest an origin at Capodimonte for the example now in Madrid.

The great masterpiece of the Capodimonte factory is the 'Porcelain-Room' erected in the Royal Villa at Portici between 1757–9. It was moved in 1865 to the Palace of Capodimonte, where it may still be seen, though the great hanging chandelier, surmounted by figures of a Chinese and a monkey clasping a palm-tree, crashed in fragments when a bomb fell near during the Second World War. The room is about 18 by 14 feet and 14 feet high. Apart from five large mirrors and one door, the walls are entirely covered with large interlocking porcelain plaques, about half an inch or more in thickness. Groups of large Chinese figures and vases, moulded in high relief, are enclosed in crimson-feathered frames whose rich rococo style may be seen in Plate 81. The flawless white material, the bright gilding and enamel colours, and the irresponsible gaiety of the Chinese figures make this one of the happiest creations of the Rococo in Europe—much surpassing the early Vienna porcelain-room constructed for Count Dubsky at Brünn about 1730. So perfect is the technique, in spite of the large scale, that a visitor who sees this room for the first time is obliged to

---

[1] The Naples example illustrated by Morazzoni, Tav. CIV (wrongly described as the work of Francesco Celebrano, of the Royal Factory); and by T. E. Romano, *Il Museo 'Duca di Martina'*, 1936, p. 59.

The Madrid group illustrated by M. Perez-Villamil, *Catalogo . . . coleccion Laiglesia*, Lam. 1.

(1) *Plate* 82.

re-adjust his whole conception of porcelain as a decorative medium. Giuseppe Gricci and his brother Stefano were the modellers; Fischer and Luigi Restile the painters. In the Villa Floridiana is a mirror with rococo porcelain frame surmounted by cupids, said to have come from this room. But a console table painted with oriental flowers and supported by a figure of a monkey (in the Musée Céramique at Sèvres) is of inferior workmanship and may have emanated from the Buen Retiro factory.

Capodimonte has well deserved its former reputation as the most distinguished of the Italian factories. In artistic quality its useful wares and figures stand high among the eighteenth-century porcelains of Europe, to which they make a unique and original contribution. They even had a modest commercial success. The experimental period was brief; sales began two years after opening, and the sale of stock continued till 1763, four years after the works had closed.

BUEN RETIRO

Though the archives of the Buen Retiro factory perished with it in 1812, some surviving documents and notices of its history have been published by Riaño and Perez Villamil. Three ships left Naples for Alicante in October 1759, laden with 44 of the Capodimonte staff, their families, and 88 tons of equipment (including $4\frac{3}{4}$ tons of porcelain-paste). A new factory, built in the grounds of the Buen Retiro Palace on the eastern outskirts of Madrid, was ready by May 1760. Giovanni Tommaso Bonicelli continued as administrative Intendant till 1781, being succeeded by his son Domingo (d. 1797). The responsible post of acting-director was held in turn by the paste-composer Gaetano Schepers (d. after 1764), by the chief modeller Giuseppe (José) Gricci (d. 1770), and by Carlos Schepers (elder son of Gaetano, d. 1783). In this year troubles long brewing in the factory came to a head. Costs had been enormous; the paste made from Spanish materials, though good for ornamental pieces, was unfit for useful wares that might be sold. There was also an inherited feud between the sons of Giuseppe Gricci and Sebastian Schepers (second son of Gaetano). It seems that each family had its own recipe for the paste; that of the Gricci contained ground flint and was very glassy, while the Schepers recipe was said to contain so much sand that it skinned the hands of the workmen. With Bonicelli's support Carlos (d. 1795) and Felipe Gricci (d. 1803) succeeded as acting-directors, and just before his death in 1788 King Charles III decided that the productions must at last be put on sale. The showroom remained open till 1800, but did little business because the objects were mainly ornamental and far too dear. Contemporary travellers observed that no visitors were admitted to the factory, presumably for fear they should see how badly it was run. Between 1798–1802 Sebastian Schepers was allowed to make experiments with a new paste. They were disastrous, and in 1803 Bartolomé Sureda, the new director, introduced with the help of two workmen from Sèvres a hard paste containing magnesite as a substitute for kaolin. He reversed the policy of the factory, making useful wares instead of ornamental pieces and figures. But work ceased when French troops occupied the building in 1808, and the minor factory restored at La Moncloa (1817–49) need not be considered here.

Buen Retiro porcelain may best be studied in Madrid. The Museo Arqueologico Nacional now houses the remains of the royal collection, with the exception of the clocks, vases, etc., still decorating the former Royal Palaces. The famous collection of Don Francisco de Laiglesia has passed to the Museo Municipal, where since a theft some years ago no one is allowed to open cases to clean the objects or take photographs. A few important pieces from the former Osma collection are in the Instituto de Valencia de Don Juan; and Doña Maria Bauzá has superb examples in her private house.

The masterpiece of the Capodimonte factory had been the Porcelain-Room at Portici, and a repetition of this was the first major work undertaken in Spain. In the Palace of Aranjuez, south of Madrid, is a porcelain-room in precisely the same style, but larger, with crimson-feathered rococo mirror-frames, groups of Chinese figures in high relief between them, and scrolled wall-chandeliers (1). There was also a great hanging chandelier shaped like a Chinese and a monkey clasping a palm-tree, which may have been taken from the same moulds as the one at Portici (this chandelier has now been removed to the porcelain-room in the Royal Palace on the western outskirts of Madrid). There is no difference whatever between the Portici and Aranjuez rooms in the quality of the beautiful white paste and rich colour, and Perez Villamil is almost certainly correct in supposing that the raw materials were imported from Italy. This might partly account for the enormous cost—571,555 Spanish reales. Conspicuously painted on a vase in relief is the signature 'JOSEPH GRICCI DELINEA[it] ET SCUL[it] 1763'; the same date appears under Charles III's monogram in the corners, and in shields on the ceiling is written 'ANO 1765', the year in which the work was probably completed.

Between 1760–70 Gricci's influence imparted to various figures and groups the same strong rococo style. In a corner of the Aranjuez room itself is a console-bracket supporting a group of massively

---

(1) *Plate* 84.

modelled infants on a high scrolled rococo base. The Museo Municipal in Madrid has a wonderful ewer and basin, with rich rococo relief-work and the bust of an infant in the round on the handle; and in the same collection is a highly ornate frame with holy water stoup, enclosing an oval painted relief of the *Noli me tangere*. These works are surely by Gricci himself, and the quality of the pure white paste suggests that they may have been made of materials imported from Italy. A heavy yellowish paste, probably made from Spanish ingredients, was used for other pieces such as the fine group in Plate 83, whose base closely resembles the frames in the Aranjuez porcelain-room. In the Madrid collections are boisterous and sturdy infants seated singly on scrolled bases, representing the Seasons (1), and the same truculent children appear as cherubs on a holy water stoup in the Victoria and Albert Museum. Rather later, perhaps after 1770, are some tall slender figures of Chinese men and women with unusually elaborate rococo scroll supports, made in a material which resembles cream-coloured earthenware rather than porcelain.

In the Royal Palace at Madrid is a second porcelain room, smaller than that at Aranjuez, and utterly different in its colder neo-classical style (2). Against the background of white panels are vases, swags, consoles with masks, and infants in the round or in high relief, with a limited colour-scheme of gold and a deep inky transparent turquoise. The paste lacks brilliance and is slightly yellow, and the over-vitreous glaze is badly crazed where it has run thick. This room cost 256,958 reales—less than half that at Aranjuez. According to notes left by Osma it bears the signature of Gaetano Schepers, but other Spanish writers take the more probable view that the work was done under the directorship of his son Carlos (1770–83). For what his statement is worth, a workman named Francesco Brancaccio, who returned from Buen Retiro to Naples in 1784 or 1786, said that there were then 'two Cabinets of porcelain in the Royal Palace of Madrid'.[1]

We may infer from the history of the factory that in the time of Carlos Schepers (1770–83) there was much trouble with the paste, and here may belong various figures and groups, some very large, made in a dull and unattractive material somewhat resembling the cream-coloured or white earthenware made in Staffordshire during the later part of the eighteenth century. The colouring is harsh and opaque, and a thin smear of neutral grey, green or purple is often spread over the usual rock-work bases as if to conceal the inferior brilliance of the paste. It is interesting to note the persistence of a Capodimonte

[1] Minieri Riccio, *Gli artefici ed i miniatori*, pp. 32, 34–5.

(1) *Plates* 86A, B; (2) *Plate* 85.

mannerism in the groups of punctures, stabbed in the interstices of the rocks to imitate moss; and a new trick of carving groups of leaves in the surface. First comes a series of peasant-groups in Spanish dress, on bases formed of rounded rocks (1); they are ponderously modelled, and lack the gaiety and sprightliness of movement of the earlier Capodimonte groups, which they may have been intended to recall. The paste of these groups is white and fairly good. Allied to the peasant groups, and in the same heavy style, are mythological or classical subjects on rockwork bases—Diana and Endymion, Prometheus and the Vulture, Cleopatra with serpents, Venus and Cupid, Andromeda bound, etc. There are some very large groups of three infants with a sheep or goat, which show the continuing influence of Gricci, though one example is signed 'CF', perhaps by the modeller Carlos Fumo. The paste of these is usually very bad. A large group of Alexander at the tomb of Achilles is so powerfully conceived that it might well be from a model left by Giuseppe Gricci (2); there are two examples in the Madrid collections, both of inferior white 'earthenware', and another in the Villa Floridiana at Naples in good white porcelain with brilliant enamel painting. Perhaps the porcelain version is the later, dating from the directorship of Carlos Gricci (1784–95). Other large groups have rectangular bases painted with marbling—Anthony and Cleopatra, and a lady handing an infant to a kneeling negro (this unexplained subject is related to another group where the negro takes refuge up a tree, while the infant in its cradle is suckled by a leopardess). Some smaller figures or groups, still on rockwork bases, are more slender in modelling and represent either classical deities such as Diana the huntress, or conversation subjects in eighteenth century dress.

There is circumstantial evidence that under Carlos Gricci (1784–95) an excellent glassy white paste came into use for ornamental vases, and groups and figures of the same material were probably made in his time. Some draw inspiration from much earlier Meissen porcelain; for example two groups of Bacchus and Ceres with infants on high rocky bases about 15 inches high (Instituto de Valencia de Don Juan), and a straight copy of Kaendler's standing figure of Bacchus as Autumn, of which the original was made in 1745 (Bauzá Collection). Figures representing the Signs of the Zodiac have low square bases and are sometimes made of a fine yellowish porcelain, like the 'Vestal Virgin' illustrated here (3). In the last quarter of the eighteenth century many figures were made in unglazed 'biscuit' porcelain. These are often unmarked, and hard to identify.

---

(1) *Plate* 86c; (2) *Plate* 87; (3) *Plate* 89a.

It should be noted that Perez Villamil has published as Buen Retiro four massive figures of children representing the Continents, each about 2 feet 9 inches in height.[1] These are in fact Chelsea porcelain of the 'red anchor mark' period (1752–8) and may still be seen in a private house in Madrid.

From the Madrid collections one gains the impression that the ornamental Buen Retiro vases which show the greatest technical accomplishment are those in a pronounced neo-classical style. They were evidently made under the regime of the two younger Gricci (1784–1803), who also produced plaques, vases, and modelled flowers in unglazed material imitating Wedgwood's 'blue jasper' ware (examples in the Royal Palace, Madrid, and in the Casita del Principe at the Escorial). A brilliant, glassy white paste was used for open bell-shaped vases on pedestal feet, or for tall slender urns primly painted with landscapes and classical figures in panels or medallions. These have clearly outlived the Capodimonte tradition. But there are earlier urn-shaped pieces whose broad, angular shoulders or almost globular forms are still reminiscent of the baroque; they often have grotesque masks at the sides, surmounted by handles in the shape of outward-curving cockle-shells (apparently not found in Capodimonte wares). They are often painted with oriental flowers of a kind already familiar at Capodimonte (I), and sometimes with battles or cupids in stippled monochrome. Most are in the dull yellow paste associated so often with Buen Retiro. But the oriental flowers remained long in favour, and when they appear on good white porcelain we must be guided by the shape of the vessel to decide whether the piece is neo-classical, and therefore Buen Retiro, or rococo, and therefore possibly Capodimonte. We have already considered the ornamental vases and other vessels with vine-stem handles (see p. 49). These form the class in which certainty of attribution is most difficult, but the balance of probability inclines towards Capodimonte.

The official documents published by Perez Villamil, no less than the witness of contemporary travellers, should convince us that before the reorganization of 1804 very few useful wares were made at Buen Retiro. Certain pieces in the Madrid collections have been claimed for Capodimonte (see page 49), and to them should perhaps be added two large dishes and a coffee-can of very white paste, loosely painted with oriental flowers and large parrots. In 1775 a richly gilt dinner-service of Sèvres porcelain was made for Prince Charles of Asturias (from 1788 King Charles IV) and his wife Luisa; its decoration

---

[1] *Artes é industrias del Buen Retiro*, Plates XVIII, XIX.

(I) *Plate* 73A.

included their linked initials, and in the border, castles in medallions and oval panels with figures in landscape. There exist many pieces copied at Buen Retiro from this service, either for replacement or augmentation; they include cups and saucers.[1] The paste of the copies is yellow and the glaze badly crazed, as might be expected during the directorship of Carlos Schepers (1770–83). Oval glass-coolers and other shapes moulded from the Sèvres service were painted with stock Buen Retiro motives such as fruit and oriental flowers. The example illustrated here (1) is of opaque white earthenware, as are a teapot with double-twist spout, and a cup and saucer, both in the Victoria and Albert Museum. There are some Buen Retiro plates painted in such minute detail that they can only have been intended for show, like fine Italian maiolica. That in Plate 88A takes its decoration, through an engraving, from one of the paintings executed by Eustache Le Sueur about 1645 for the *Chambre des Muses* in the Hotel Lambert de Thorigny, Paris.[2] It is interesting that here, as at Le Nove,[3] porcelain-painters of the 'neo-classical' period had recourse to the designs of French 'classical' masters of the seventeenth century. Such cups and saucers as survive are mostly in a pronounced neo-classical style, cylindrical in shape—indeed, many of them bear the red mark 'Md' under a crown which was introduced under Sureda's direction in 1803.

Buen Retiro was a disappointing factory to all concerned, as is freely admitted by its able historian Perez Villamil. Transplanted to an uncongenial soil, the Capodimonte tradition soon withered and there was nothing original to take its place. Charles III must have envied the competence of the new factory started by his son Ferdinand at Naples.

NAPLES: THE ROYAL FACTORY (1771–1806)

Ferdinand IV of Naples has left in history a name compound of odium and ridicule. His long reign from 1759–1825 was twice interrupted by periods of exile in Palermo; the first in 1798–9, when for eight months Naples was in the hands of native revolutionaries or French troops; the second from 1806, when Joseph Bonaparte till 1808 and Joachim Murat until 1815 occupied his throne. Lack of education and intellect reduced his serious interests to hunting,

---

[1] Part of the Sèvres service survives in the Museo Arqueologico Nacional. A Buen Retiro plate copied from it is in the Fitzwilliam Museum, Cambridge.

[2] L. Dimier, *Histoire de la peinture française du retour de Vouet à la mort de Lebrun*, Tome II, 1927, Plate IV.

[3] See p. 23.

(1) *Plate* 89B.

fishing and buffoonery. But in 1768 he married Maria Carolina, the ambitious and scheming daughter of the Empress Maria Theresa; and she ensured close political relations with Austria. Ferdinand showed dutiful respect to his father Charles III of Spain until 1784, when a family misunderstanding was smoothed out through the good offices of Sir William Hamilton, British Minister in Naples since 1764. Hamilton's diplomatic task was to prevent any *rapprochement* between Naples and France. Queen Maria Carolina needed no encouragement to hate the French revolutionaries after they had beheaded her sister Marie Antoinette (1793); Nelson easily obtained the collaboration of Neapolitan troops on his first short visit to Naples in that year; and when he re-appeared after the victory of the Nile in 1798 he was received with open arms, especially by Lady Hamilton, now the confidante of the Queen. For their flight to Palermo the Royal Family preferred Nelson's flagship to that of the Admiral Prince Caracciolo, and the British representatives fully shared the guilt for the ferocious reprisals against the rebels after the return to Naples in 1799.

Since the discovery there of antique statues by the Prince d'Elboeuf in 1711, Naples had attracted the curiosity of scholars and collectors; but serious excavations at Herculaneum did not begin until 1738, under King Charles. They were conducted in secrecy, as a royal preserve; and the finds first became generally known through the official publication in 1757 of *Le pitture antiche d'Ercolano e contorni incise con qualche spiegazione—tomo primo*. Six further volumes with illustrations appeared between 1762–79. Meanwhile the great German archaeologist J. J. Winckelmann had been sent by Augustus III of Saxony to report on the finds; he was not tactful, and in 1762 published his first *Letter* strongly criticising the conduct of the excavations. After 1763 work was concentrated on the newly identified site of Pompeii. Sir William Hamilton became an enthusiast for classical antiquities, selling two great collections formed in Naples to the British Museum (1772) and to Thomas Hope (1798); he also promoted the illustrated publications of ancient Greek and South Italian vases by 'd'Hancarville' (P. F. Hughes, 1766–7) and W. Tischbein (1791). Plates from the former work reached the hands of Josiah Wedgwood soon after printing, and helped to establish the neo-classical style in English ceramics.

In decreeing the revival of a Royal Porcelain Factory in November 1771, Ferdinand IV evidently wished to follow his father's example (work at Capodimonte had ceased twelve years before). The Marchese Brigadiere Ricci directed the preparation of quarters near the Royal Villa at Portici; but in June 1772 he died and was succeeded by Tomas

Perez, a Spaniard. In the same month it was decided to build a new factory on the north side of the Royal Palace in Naples itself, beside the harbour, and thither the staff moved from Portici in 1773. The composition of the paste was entrusted to Gaetano Tucci (d. 1780), an old Capodimonte hand; Francesco Celebrano, a pupil of Solimena, was chief modeller until 1781; and the painters included Antonio Cioffi, who had worked at Capodimonte, and Saverio Maria Grue, a member of a family long connected with the manufacture of painted maiolica at Castelli in the Abruzzi. At first the factory was small: Perez recommended an increase of staff in 1774 and deplored the lack of original invention. But he died in 1779, and it was his able successor Domenico Venuti who, first as Director and subsequently as Intendant, raised the factory to importance and gave it its typically neo-classical stamp. On Venuti's suggestion an Academy of the Nude was founded in 1781; Filippo Taglioni was called from the Imperial Viennese Factory to become chief modeller; and a new kiln was constructed by Magnus Fessler, also from Vienna. From 1782 began the practice of making large services as diplomatic gifts to foreign courts. They included centre-pieces of biscuit-porcelain with figures devised at the Academy of the Nude. This biscuit material was curiously enough first referred to in the records of 1782 as *creta all' inglese*— 'English clay'—perhaps in confusion with cream-coloured earthenware, which was undoubtedly an English invention. It is difficult to believe that English biscuit porcelain was then known in Naples. The kiln operator promoted to compose the new paste was Giovanni Lorenzi—possibly a relation of the Pietro Lorenzi whose discoveries were adopted earlier at the Le Nove factory (see p. 20). Thanks to the documents quoted by Minieri Riccio and Morazzoni, a good deal is known about the workmen at the factory and about the important services ordered there for diplomatic purposes. The wares were put on public sale from 1779. After the Revolution of 1798–9 the factory was found to be heavily in debt, and Venuti had to surrender his monopoly of control. Joseph Napoleon sold the factory in 1807 to the French firm Jean Poulard Prad and Company, and the works were removed to the suppressed convent of Santa Maria della Vita, at the foot of the Capodimonte hill. Here they soon declined; Poulard Prad and his partners embarked on litigation among themselves; and work had ceased long before 1834, when the effects were finally sold and the building converted into a cholera-hospital. On his second restoration in 1815 King Ferdinand, now styled Ferdinand I, showed no further interest in porcelain. Maria Carolina was dead and he had morganatically married the buxom but mature Duchess of Floridia, mother of six sons. By an odd chance the home he prepared and named for her on the Rione Vomero high above Naples has now become the most beautiful museum of ceramics in Europe.

The mark used by the factory from the beginning was the monogram 'F R F' (*Fabbrica Reale Ferdinandea*), painted in blue, red or black enamel under a crown. 'N' under a crown, painted in underglaze blue or stamped in the paste, was apparently adopted about the end of the eighteenth century, and was also fraudulently used at Doccia and elsewhere from the mid-nineteenth century onwards (see p. 40).

The porcelain is a highly translucent glassy soft-paste evidently akin to that formerly made at Capodimonte. Early pieces often show defects and are distinctly yellowish. An opaque white tin-glaze was applied to some of the fine services made after 1782, but this was abandoned as the paste itself improved to a pure white or pleasant creamy tone. The gilding is thick and apt to wear off; a special peculiarity is the occasional use of burnished gilding in two or even three contrasted tints—yellow, coppery, and greenish (1). In 1806 two painters were given a gratuity for an improved and cheaper method of gilding, which may perhaps be identified on pieces where it is thinner but more extensively applied, especially on knobs and handles. There seems to be no real evidence for a common assumption that the factory in its later stages also made cream-coloured earthenware.

Between 1771 and the appointment of Venuti in 1779 the style followed in table-wares was a late and enfeebled rococo, groping back to the Capodimonte tradition. A saucer dated 1772 must have been made before the transfer from Portici (2); it is painted with a fantastic purple landscape in a frame of orange and gold, and the paste is blistered and discoloured. A heavy flower-holder of deep cream-coloured paste also shows fire-cracks (3); and there is discolouration due to misfiring on the back of a plate with richly gilt border and a family group in finely stippled pale colours (4). Coarsely stippled fruit recalling a favourite Capodimonte motive is seen on two marked saucers in the Victoria and Albert Museum, whose technical defects suggest an early date; and there are plates and other pieces with careful flower-painting in pale, pleasant colours that again recall Capodimonte. The compact shape of the covered bowl in Plate 90B may be compared with that of its more sprawling predecessor, Plate 70B; there is more tidiness too, in the exquisitely painted decoration. Small painted busts of Orientals or Europeans (5), and painted figures of classical deities or Seasons (6) seem to retain enough rococo

---

(1) *Plate* 92B; (2) *Plate* 90A; (3) *Plate* 91B; (4) *Plate* 91A; (5) *Plate* 95A, B. A similar pair has the 'F.R.F.' mark. (6) *Plate* 94B.

feeling for some of them to belong to the same early period. But there is no apparent ground for Morazzoni's attribution to Francesco Celebrano of the splendid white group in the Villa Floridiana, showing the Virgin and St. John mourning over the dead Christ; it and its coloured counterpart in Madrid have already been mentioned as works of Giuseppe Gricci (p. 51). In 1779 King Ferdinand felt sufficiently pleased with his porcelain to send a case of it to his father in Spain.

The radical change of taste due to Venuti became evident in 1781, when work began on a service of 88 pieces which was sent to the Spanish court in the following year, accompanied by the artists who had painted it. This was the 'Herculaneum Service'; it comprised as centre-pieces modelled busts of Seneca, Scipio, Pallas, Jupiter Ammon etc., and a biscuit group of Charles III exhorting his son Ferdinand to pursue the excavations. Venuti caused to be printed a book with engravings illustrating and explaining the subjects represented. The service has apparently been dispersed; to it may have belonged a number of plates and coolers painted on a tin-glazed ground with subjects like that on our Plate 92B, taken from ancient wall-paintings. The light fret border of this very pleasing service is punctuated by cameo heads in medallions inscribed 'Museo Farnesiano'. (Charles III had inherited through his mother Elisabetta, the last survivor of the Farnese family, their famous collection of ancient sculpture; in the reign of Ferdinand IV this collection, together with the finds from Herculaneum and Pompeii, was rehoused in the building now named the Museo Nazionale in Naples.) The plate from a similar service here illustrated (1) has a border in relief, and birds in bronze and yellow tones of tooled gold. The figure subjects are taken from the engravings in Le pitture antiche d'Ercolano, and inscriptions on the reverse commonly quote volume and plate-number; thus this figure of a youth is after a wall-painting found at Gragnano (the ancient Stabiae) illustrated in Vol. IV, Plate xxx, published in 1765.

An 'Etruscan Service' of 282 pieces, started in 1785, was two years later despatched to England in charge of the modeller Taglioni and of John Chisel (or Casely), an Englishman employed as a painter in the factory between 1771 and 1804. Like the Herculaneum Service, it was 'explained' by Venuti in a book;[1] though the book was hardly necessary in view of the long descriptions inscribed on the vessels

[1] D. Venuti: *Interpretation des peintures dessinées sur une service de table travaillé d'après la bosse dans la Royale Fabrique de Porcellaine, par ordre de Sa Majesté le Roi des Deux Siciles*. 179 engravings. Naples, 1787 (100 copies were printed, and five more on Holland paper; a copy is in the Library of the Victoria and Albert Museum).

(1) *Plate* 92B.

themselves. The soup-dishes, tureens, compotiers and so on are rather tastelessly adapted from ancient Greek or South Italian vases in the red-figure or black-figure styles (1); and the plates are painted on a tin-glazed ground with recognisable 'portraits' of actual vases found at Nola and elsewhere in the Kingdom of Naples (2). Many pieces bear the monogram mark 'FRF' under a crown, painted in red. A great part of the service can still be seen in the China Museum at Windsor Castle, though not Taglioni's centre-piece in biscuit porcelain, which represented Tarchon, King of the Etruscans, presiding over gladiatorial contests. The 'Etruscan Service' is of interest not only as a pedantic curiosity, but also as a historical document. In 1779 the re-organisation of the Neapolitan Navy was entrusted to John Francis Edward Acton, an expatriate Anglo-Irishman who later became Prime Minister of Naples and inherited an English baronetcy. Acton needed the secrets of English naval construction, and hoped that a handsome gift to King George III would open doors for his agents. The Etruscan Service was conveyed to England in the Neapolitan warships Ceres and Minerva, whose commander, the Cavaliere Fortiguerri, obtained permission to visit Woolwich Arsenal and Deptford Docks, but was less lucky at Portsmouth.[1]

The records give the dates of many services with subjects other than classical, and of course there survive many less important pieces of which there is no record. Hunting-scenes are mentioned in 1782; animals in landscape 1783–4; views in the Kingdom of Naples, including eruptions of Vesuvius, 1785–7; figures in local peasant dress, 1784 (3); warships; birds; and fish after book-illustrations by Catesby. They are usually shown in oval or round medallions, with light and graceful wreath or Pompeian fret borders; but one service has land-scapes in purple vignette. The shapes, such as the trefoil-mouthed jug in Plate 93A, are often more literally copied from the antique than are those of other contemporary factories. Fussy gilt borders, hard realistic painting, and elaborately modelled handles and knobs appear as the 'neo-classical' style gives place to the 'Empire' about 1800.

Biscuit-porcelain figures of the late eighteenth century are today commonly regarded with distaste, but the visitor to Capodimonte may still wonder at Taglioni's huge group, some five feet high, of Jupiter striking down the Titans. It was modelled before 1787. There is also a charming series of figures for a table centre—Aurora in her chariot, escorted by the dancing Muses. Camillo Celebrano and other

[1] Morazzoni quotes extensively from the Naples State Archives. Fanny Burney (Madame D'Arblay) saw the service and centrepieces in October 1787, and has left an accurate description of them (Memoirs, Vol. III, p. 449).

(1) *Plate* 96B; (2) *Plate* 96A; (3) *Plate* 93.

modellers continued making biscuit figures after the factory was taken over by Poulard Prad in 1806; there are some large portrait busts of the Murat family.

Of more interest are some very lively and well-modelled figures and groups in the respectable middle-class dress of the late eighteenth century (1), which appear in both glazed and unglazed biscuit porcelain and when glazed usually bear the crowned 'N' mark. One coloured example in the British Museum, a lady with a book under her arm, bears the incised signature 'P' over 'Giordano'. A modeller named Michele Giordano worked at the Royal Factory from 1789 till his death in 1799 and may have been the artist who created the type, but the 'P' is puzzling and has given rise to unconvincing explanations. Eisner de Eisenhof affirmed that it referred to the painter Gennaro Paterno, but quoted no authority for this man's particular association with Giordano. An otherwise untrustworthy catalogue of an Exhibition held at Naples in 1877 gives the name of Giuseppe Giordano, called 'Peppe', as a modeller; but the name is not recorded by Minieri Riccio, though an Antonio Giordano was a colour-grinder in 1779–80 and a Giosué Giordano a lowly-paid hand in 1803. There exist many unmarked figures of the same general type both in biscuit porcelain and in glazed cream-coloured earthenware. The latter were probably made outside the Royal Factory. In 1794 two factory modellers, P. P. Acquaviva and Antonio Sorrentino, were imprisoned for making and selling biscuit porcelain in their own homes. And before the end of the eighteenth century the manufacture of cream-coloured earthenware, perhaps including figures, had been firmly established in Naples by the rival firms of Giustiniani and Del Vecchio.

It should be added that Poulard Prad, at some time after 1807, began decorating in Naples hard-paste porcelain imported from France 'in the white'. This practice was continued by Raffaele Giovine and his workshop from 1826 until 1860. With their unsympathetic material, brassy gilding, and facile painting of views, peasants, and military subjects, these wares have as little artistic value as those decorated about the same time by Feuillet in Paris.

*   *   *

Two minor factories in ROME should not pass without mention. Captain Filippo Coccumos obtained in 1761 from the Reverenda Camera Apostolica a privilege for making porcelain statues, jugs, cups and saucers. On the Festival of Sts. Paul and Peter he was to present to the Camera Apostolica a figure of a saint. Only two examples of his work survive; a Deposition from the Cross, seen and described by

(1) *Plates* 94A, C; 95C.

Fortnum, and a figure of St. Anthony of Padua, formerly in Baron Eisner de Eisenhof's possession in Vienna. Both are of biscuit porcelain, and bear the incised mark 'ROMA I MAG 1769' with crossed 'CC' under a crown. The initials are those of Carlo Coccorese, a former Capodimonte workman who fell ill on the journey to Spain in 1759 and turned back to try his fortune in Rome. He left Coccumos in 1769, and the factory closed in or soon after 1781.

The other Roman factory was started in 1785 by the Venetian Giovanni Volpato, better known as the founder of a school of engravers who reproduced works by the Old Masters. It continued after Volpato's death (1803) and that of his son Giuseppe (1805) until about 1818, when his grandson Angelo gave it up in preference for the earthenware factory run by the family at Cività Castellana. The chief products were figures and groups in biscuit-porcelain, after contemporary sculpture by Antonio Canova or showing Italian peasants in regional dress. The mark is 'G. Volpato Roma' impressed, often followed by the date.

MARKS

MEDICI PORCELAIN, FLORENCE (1575–87)

(*See also pages* 3–6)

(1)

(2)   (3)

(1) On the gourd, *Plate* 2c. (Indicating that this was a trial piece.)
About 1575. Other early pieces are unmarked.

(2) On a ewer in the Baron Robert de Rothschild Collection, date-
able 1575–8. The initials stand for 'Franciscus Medicis Magnus Dux
Etruriae Secundus'. A dish in the Metropolitan Museum has carefully painted on the back, filling the whole space inside the foot-ring,
the six balls of the Medici arms, inscribed 'F.M.M. . . .' (the rest
illegible), and over them a Grand-ducal crown. On a small ewer in the
Musée du Louvre are five circles inscribed 'F.M.M.E.D.'.

(3) The dome of Santa Maria del Fiore, the Cathedral of Florence,
accompanied by the letter 'F'. This appears to have been adopted as

F   65

the regular mark between 1578–87. It is drawn large in a variety of forms, according to the fancy of the artist.

All these marks are in the same underglaze blue as the painted decoration.

PADUA

(See also page 6)

(1) (2)

(3)

(1) On a bowl in the Victoria and Albert Museum (*Plate* 4A); (2) and (3) on another bowl in the same Museum. Painted in blackish blue.

VENICE, VEZZI FACTORY (1720–7)

(See also pages 8–13)

(1)
incised

(2)
in underglaze
blue

(3)
in underglaze
blue

(4)
in underglaze
blue

(5)
in underglaze blue,
and red, blue, or
gold enamel

(6)
in red or
underglaze blue

(7)
in red, green, or
blue

V̇èn·

(8)

in red

V̇≐a

(9)

in red or gold

Ven.ᵃ A. G. 1726.

(10)

in red

Lodouico Orrolani Venciu dipinse nella Fabrica d. Porcelana in Venetiu·

(11)

in crimson

(1) On the cup and saucer, *Plate* 8B.

(2), (3) and (4) On wares painted in underglaze blue; (2) is on the teapot, *Plate* 6A.

(5), (6), (8), (9) The commonest marks, usually in red.

(7) The flourished 'V' is sometimes very fanciful; on one recorded piece there are monsters' heads at the ends of the letter.

(10) On the saucer, *Plate* 13B.

(11) On the saucer, *Plate* 10C.

The painted marks are often accompanied by capital or lower case letters of unknown meaning, incised in the paste.

VENICE, HEWELCKE FACTORY (1758–63)

(See also pages 14–16)

deeply incised and painted red

Existing pieces probably date from 1761–3. The portrait-plaque in *Plate* 15A, dated 1763, has a letter 'V' in relief under the head.

ITALIAN PORCELAIN

VENICE, COZZI FACTORY (1764–1812)
(*See also pages* 16–20)

Nella Fabbrica
Del Sig.: Geminiano
Cozzi
li 3i Maggio 1765
L. O.

in red

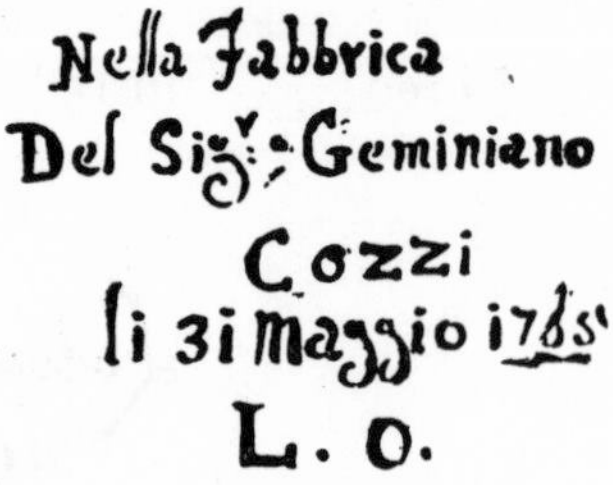

The factory-mark of an anchor, always too roughly and boldly drawn to be mistaken for that of Chelsea, seems to have been adopted in 1766. It is absent on the coffee-pot dated 1765 (*Plate* 18B), and the saucer of 1765 whose inscription is given above (*see page* 17, note 1). The initials on this piece, which belongs to Dr. Ducret, are those of the painter Lodovico Ortolani the younger, who also worked at Le Nove; the writing may be contrasted with that of the elder L. Ortolani, who worked a generation earlier at the Vezzi factory (*see page* 67, No. 11).

The anchor mark is sometimes accompanied by letters of unknown meaning, perhaps referring to an owner or consignment (G.M., I.G., V.F.).

LE NOVE (1762–1825)
(*See also pages* 20–25)

(1)	(2)	(3)	(4)
		Noue . AntonioBon	Nove
		in purple	in relief

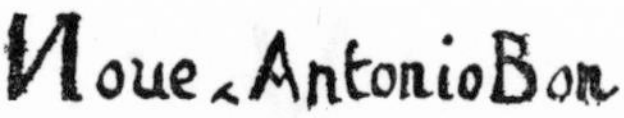

(5)	(6)	(7)	(8)
✳	✳	*Nove*	Nove ✳
in red, blue or gold		incised	in gold

(9)

in gold

(10)

in red

(11)

(12)

in gold

(13)

in gold

(14)   (15)

incised

(1) and (2) Incorporated in the design, on two plates in the Sèvres Museum (*Plate* 28A). The monogram of Giovanni Battista Antonibon who founded the pottery at Le Nove in 1728. The plates themselves date from 1762.

(3) About 1762; on a teapot in the Sèvres Museum which also bears the GAB monogram.

(4) Very indistinctly moulded, on wares made in rococo style by Pasquale Antonibon between 1763–73. (*Plate* 30A).

(5) and (6) The normal factory-mark from 1781 onwards, but probably also used before 1773. Commonest in red. The crossed strokes are often roughly drawn, and do not give the star a solid centre as at Doccia.

(7) Roughly incised on figures and groups made after 1781.

(8) After 1781.

(9) On the jardinière, *Plate* 31. The signature of the painter Giovanni Marcon (or Marconi) is sometimes incorporated in the design (*Plate* 32).

(10) Found with or without the star, on cups and saucers of about 1800. Probably an owner's mark. Through a misunderstanding it has sometimes been stated that the Cozzi factory also used this mark.

(11) Incorporated in the design; Baroni period (1801–25). (*Plate* 35).

(12) Baroni period (1801–25). Probably an owner's mark. (On a *décor bois* cup and saucer in the Sèvres Musem, accompanied by marks (5) and (14).

(13) Baroni period (1801–25). Probably an owner's mark.

(14) and (15) Scratched roughly in the paste; late eighteenth and early nineteenth centuries.

TURIN (about 1737–43)
(*See also page* 29)

The cross of Savoy and the GR monogram initials of Giorgio Giacinto Rossetti are incised on two small busts, accompanied by 'TORINO' painted in underglaze blue. (Turin, Museo Civico). No other examples have been identified.

VISCHE (1755–6)
(*See also page* 29)

impressed

VINOVO (1776–1820)
(*See also pages* 29–31)

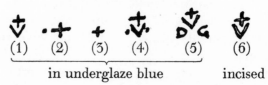

The cross from the Arms of Savoy, and the initial of the place-name. The initials on No. (5) are those of Dr. Gioanetti, who directed the factory from 1780–96 and again when it re-opened in 1815. Of other initials found with the mark, 'L' is that of Lomello, Director 1815–20; 'CA' are those of the painters Carasso or Carpano, whose name sometimes appears in full.

DOCCIA (1735–present day)

(See also pages 32–44)

(1)	(2)	(3)	(4)	(5)	(6)	(7)
in red, blue, or gold			impressed	in red	in blue crimson or purple	in green

(8)	(9)	(10)
in red	incised	incised

GI	GIN	GINORI	
(11)	(12)	(13)	(14)
impressed			in blue, or impressed

The star is taken from the Arms of Ginori. It has a more solid centre than the star used at Le Nove. Early pieces are unmarked. (1) to (3) Late eighteenth and first half of nineteenth century. (4) Accompanied by a painted gold star, on a cup and saucer with Italian views (Victoria and Albert Museum, about 1792–1800). (5) to (8) On useful wares and figures with the tin-glaze, about 1770–90.

(9) On wares of the finest paste, 1792–1815. (e.g. *Plate* 53B).

(10) With a red star, on a cup painted with Greek figures in the Victoria and Albert Museum, about 1810.

(11) to (13) Nineteenth-century marks.

(14) On the so-called 'Capodimonte reproduction' relief-wares; second half of the nineteenth century.

CAPODIMONTE (1743–59)

(See also pages 46–52)

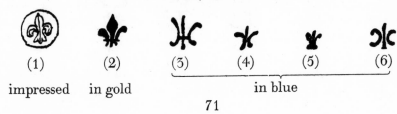

(1)	(2)	(3)	(4)	(5)	(6)
impressed	in gold		in blue		

(1) On figures and groups certainly made at Capodimonte; also on two large table-wares whose attribution between late Capodimonte and early Buen Retiro is less certain. This mark appears not to have been used on figures made at Buen Retiro.

(2) On an especially fine tea-service of about 1745 in the Victoria and Albert Museum (*Plate* 66, 67c).

(3) to (6) Roughly drawn and often smudged by the glaze, on useful wares and occasionally on figures. Also used on Buen Retiro wares and figures.

BUEN RETIRO (1760–1808)
(*See also pages 52–7*)

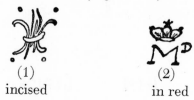

(1)	(2)
incised	in red

The marks given under Capodimonte, Nos. (3) to (6), are also those normally used on vessels and figures made at Buen Retiro.

(1) Recorded as a mark on a large group.

(2) Used in the last period of Buen Retiro under Sureda's director-ship (1804–8); also on porcelain made at La Moncloa from 1817–49. The name 'MADRID' also occurs in full.

Initials, conjecturally those of various artists, and numerals and incised signs sometimes accompany the factory-mark. A service of Berlin porcelain, painted with Spanish views and marked with the usual sceptre in blue, has led to the mistaken view that this mark was also used at Buen Retiro (it is in the Museo Arqueologico Nacional, Madrid).

NAPLES, ROYAL FACTORY (1771–1806)
(*See also pages 57–63*)

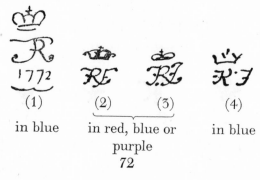

(1)	(2)	(3)	(4)
in blue	in red, blue or purple		in blue

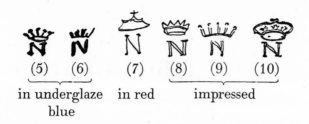

(11)
incised

(12)
in red

(1) On the saucer, *Plate* 90A, made at Portici before the move to Naples in 1773.

(2) to (4) F.R.F. monogram (for 'Fabbrica Reale Ferdinandea'), used from 1773 till 1787 or later (it occurs on the Windsor Service, *Plate* 96).

(5) to (10) Date of introduction uncertain, but the crowned 'N' seems to have superseded the 'FRF' mark in the later years of the factory.

(11) On glazed and 'biscuit' figures in popular style, late eighteenth century. Signature perhaps of the modeller Michele Giordano (d. 1799), or of the ill-documented Giuseppe (Peppe) Giordano.

(12) On hard paste porcelain imported from France and painted in Naples by Raffaele Giovine, 1826–60.

SELECT BIBLIOGRAPHY

GENERAL WORKS

J. MARRYAT, *A history of pottery and porcelain.* 3rd edition. London, 1868.

E. HANNOVER, *Pottery and porcelain. A handbook for collectors,* vol. III, *European porcelain.* English edition by B. Rackham, London, 1925.

U. OJETTI and others, *Il settecento italiano,* vol. II. Milan, 1932.

GIUSEPPE MORAZZONI, *Le porcellane italiane.* Milan-Rome, 1935. (The most important book, richly illustrated, but rare and very expensive.)

T. ELENA ROMANO, *Il Museo 'Duca di Martina' nella Villa 'La Floridiana' di Napoli.* Rome, 1936.

W. B. HONEY, *European ceramic art: a dictionary of factories, artists, technical terms et cetera.* London, 1952.

M. OLIVAR DAYDÍ, *La porcelana en Europa,* vol. II. Barcelona, 1953.

MEDICI PORCELAIN

BARON DAVILLIER, *Les origines de la porcelaine en Europe.* Paris, 1882.

G. GUASTI, *Di Cafaggiolo e d'altre fabbriche di ceramica in Toscana.* Florence, 1902.

B. RACKHAM. Two seicento bowls (*Burlington Magazine,* XVII, 1910, p. 163).

Paduan maiolica of the so-called 'Candiana' type (*Op. cit.,* LXVIII, 1936, p. 113).

G. LIVERANI, *Catalogo delle porcellane dei Medici.* Faenza, 1936. (Excellent survey with full bibliography.)

VENETIAN FACTORIES

W. R. DRAKE, *Notes on Venetian ceramics.* London, 1868.

G. M. URBANI DE GHELTOF. *Studi intorno alla ceramica veneziana.* Venice, 1876.

La manifattura di maiolica e di porcellana in Este. Venice, 1876.

SELECT BIBLIOGRAPHY

C. BARONI, *Le ceramiche di Nove di Bassano*. Venice, 1932.

N. BARBANTINI, *Le porcellane di Venezia e delle Nove*. Venice, 1936. (Well-illustrated catalogue of an exhibition at the Ca' Rezzonico, but with many incorrect attributions.)

G. BARIOLI, *Catalogo della I mostra di ceramiche antiche di Bassano, delle Nove, e di Vicenza*. Venice, 1954. (Exhibition at Bassano, Museo Civico.)

VINOVO

G. VIGNOLA. *Sulle maioliche e porcellane del Piemonte*. Turin, 1878.

L. DE-MAURI, *Vinovo e le sue porcellane*. Milan, 1923.

V. VIALE, *I Musei Civici nel 1932*. Turin, 1932.

DOCCIA

C. LORENZINI, *La manifattura delle porcellane di Doccia*. Florence, 1861.
   La manifattura Ginori à Doccia. Florence, 1867.

Società Ceramica Richard-Ginori, Primo Trentennio, *Memorial publication*. Florence, 1903.

G. MORAZZONI, Le porcellane di Doccia (*Dedalo*, III, 1922–3, pp. 450, 523).

CAPODIMONTE AND NAPLES

C. MINIERI RICCIO. *Gli artefici ed i miniatori della Real Fabbrica della porcellana di Napoli*.
   La Fabbrica della porcellana in Napoli e le sue vicende.
   Delle porcellane della Real Fabbrica di Napoli, delle vendite fattene e delle loro tariffe. Naples, 1878.
   (All containing valuable extracts from the Neapolitan State Records.)

A. DE EISNER EISENHOF, *Le porcellane di Capodimonte*. Milan, 1925. (Unreliable.)

BUEN RETIRO

J. F. RIAÑO. *Spanish arts*. (South Kensington Museum Handbook, London, 1879.)

M. PEREZ VILLAMIL. *Artes é industrias del Buen Retiro*. Madrid, 1904.
   Catàlogo de la coleccion de porcelanas del Buen Retiro del Excmo. Señor D. Francisco de Laiglesia. Madrid, 1908.

J. AINAUD DE LASARTE. *Ars Hispaniae X: ceramica y vidrio*. Madrid, 1952.

INDEX

'A.G.' mark, 69
anchor-mark, 17, 44, 68
Angarano, 28
Antonibon, Giovanni Battista, 14, 69
Antonibon, Pasquale, 14, 15, 20, 69
Antonio, Maestro, alchemist, 2
Anreiter von Zirnfeld, Anton, 33, 35
Anreiter von Zirnfeld, J. Carl Wende-
  lin, 33, 34, 35
Aquaviva, P. P., 63
Aranjuez, 51, 53, 54
Arduini, G. B., 1
Aue (Saxony), clay from, 9, 10
Augustus II of Saxony and Poland, 45

Baccin, G. M., 20
Baroni, Giovanni, 21, 23, 69, 70
Bassano, 14
Bertolini, glassmakers, 14
biscuit-porcelain, 27, 31, 43, 55, 62,
  63, 64
blanc-de-chine (Fukien porcelain) imi-
  tated, 11, 34, 47
'Blue Jasper' imitations, 40, 56
blue-and-white, Chinese, 1, 2
blue-and-white, Doccia, 34
blue-and-white, Medici porcelain, 3–7
blue-and-white, Venice, 11
Bohne, Ernst, 44
Bologna, 20, 25
Bonicelli, Domingo, 52
Bonicelli, Giovanni Tommaso, 52
Boselli, Jacopo, 31
Bosello, Domenico, 21, 24
Böttger, J. F., 8, 9
Boucher, 27
Brodel, G. V., 29, 30
Brongniart, Alexandre, 17, 30
Brunello, G. B., 20, 25
Bruschi, Gaspare, 33
Bruschi, Giuseppe, 33
Buen Retiro, 45, 52–7, 72
Buontalenti, Bernardo, 3

Callot, J., 16
Camillo da Urbino, 2, 5
Canova, Antonio, 64
Capodimonte, 38, 39, 45–52, 56, 59,
  71
Carlo Emmanuele of Savoy and Sar-
  dinia, 29
Carpano, painter, 31, 70
Caselli, Giovanni, 46, 48
Caselli, Maria, 47
Castelli, 59
Celebrano, Camillo, 62
Celebrano, Francesco, 59, 61
Charles III of Bourbon, King of Naples
  and Spain, 45, 49, 52, 53, 58, 61
Chelsea porcelain, 56
Chinese porcelain, 1, 2, 5, 13, 18
chinoiseries, 11, 18, 19, 23, 24, 37, 47,
  48, 51, 53, 54
Chisel, John, 61
Cioffi, Antonio, 59
Coalport, 40
Coccorese, Carlo, 64
Coccumos, Filippo, 63, 64
Commedia dell' Arte (Italian Com-
  edy), 18, 19, 41, 50
Costa, Antonio, 26
Cozzi, Geminiano, 15, 16, 17
cream-coloured earthenware, 17, 20,
  23, 24, 25, 26, 54, 55
crowned 'N' mark, 33, 40, 60, 62, 71,
  73
Cyfflé, Paul-Louis, 31

Del Vecchio, F., 63
deutsche Blumen, 35
Doccia, 7, 13, 17, 20, 24, 32, 46, 60,
  71
dome, mark, 6, 65
Du Paquier, C. I., 9, 33

Edelink, engraver, 23
'EE', mark, 71

77

Empire style, 23
Este, 15, 20, 25

'F', mark, 37, 71
Fabris, Fiorina, 25, 26
Faenza, 3, 7
Fanciullacci, G. B., 37
Farnese collection, 61
Ferdinand IV of Naples, 45, 57, 58, 59, 61
Ferrara, 2, 5
Ferriol, Charles de, 42
Fessler, Magnus, 59
Fialetti, O., 59
Fischer, Johann Sigismund, 20, 46, 52
fleur-de-lis mark, 44, 46, 48, 49, 50, 71, 72
Florence, 1, 2, 3–7, 32, 65
Fontana, Flaminio, 3
forgeries, 12, 13, 20
Franchini, Gerolamo, 25, 26
Frankenthal, 29, 30
'F.R.F.' mark, 60, 62, 72
Fumo, Carlos, 55
Fumo, Gaetano, 47

'GAB' mark, 21, 22, 68
'G.B.' mark, 21, 24, 69
Genoa, 31
'G.G.P.F.' mark, 6, 7, 66
'GI.' mark, 71
gilding, 11, 13, 18, 21, 36, 40, 50, 60, 61
Ginori, Carlo, 32, 42
Ginori, Leopoldo Carlo, 40
Ginori, Lorenzo I., 33, 36, 39
Gioanetti, V. A., 30, 70
Giordano, Giuseppe (Peppe), 63, 73
Giordano, Michele, 63, 73
Giorgio, Ambrogio di, 47
Giovine, Raffaele, 63, 73
Giustiniani, potters, 63
glass, Venetian, 2, 14
Gravelot, H., 37
Gricci, Carlos, 52, 55, 56
Gricci, Felipe, 52
Gricci, Giuseppe, 46, 47, 51–5, 61
Gricci, Stefano, 52
Grue, Saverio Maria, 59
Gussoni, Andrea, 3

Hamilton, Sir William, 58
Hannong, Pierre-Antoine, 29, 30
Helchis, Jacobus, 29, 46
Herculaneum, 45, 58, 61
Hewelcke, N. F., 14–16, 67
Hunger, C. C., 9, 13

'I.G.P.F.', mark, 6, 7, 66
Isnik, see Turkish pottery

Japanese 'Imari' decoration, 36

Le Brun, C., 23
Legrand, A., 26
Le Nove, 13–15, 20–5, 68, 69
Le Sueur, Eustache, 57
Lomello, Giovanni, 30
Lorenzo, Giovanni, 59
Lorenzo, Pietro, 20

Madrid, 45, 52, 72
magnesite, 53
maiolica, 2, 3, 7, 14, 17, 20
Marcon, Giovanni, 21, 23, 69
Marco Polo, 1
Maria Carolina of Naples, 58, 59
Maria Theresa, 32, 38, 58
'Md.' mark, 57, 72
Medici, Cosimo I de', 3
Medici, Ferdinando I de', 4
Medici, Francesco I de', 3–6, 65
Medici, Gian Gastone de', 32
Medici, Lorenzo de', 1, 3
Medici porcelain, 3–7, 65
Meissen porcelain, 8–10, 13
Meissen influence, 22, 36, 42, 46–8, 50, 55
Michelangelo, 32, 43
Modena, 25
Moncloa, La, 53, 72
Monnet, C., 26

Naples, 45, 57–63, 72
Nelson, Lord, 58
Neo-Classical style, 18, 19, 22, 37, 56, 57, 59, 61
Nicoli, Nicolao, 30
Niderviller, 30

Ortolani, Lodovico, 12, 17, 67, 68

Padua, 6, 66

Parolin, Francesco, 20, 22
Pastorino, 5
Paterno, Gennaro, 62
Pencz, G., 5
Perez, Tomas, 58, 59
Peringer, Leonardo, 2
Permoser, Balthasar, 42
Persian pottery, 5
Pier Maria da Faenza, 3
Pillement, 37
Pisa, 4
Polo, Marco, 1
Pompeii, 58
Porta, Guglielmo della, 38
Portici, 51, 58–60
Poterat, Louis, 7
Poulard Prad, 45, 59, 62, 63
'PS' mark, 37

Raphael, 5
Restile, Luigi, 46, 52
Ricci, Brigadiere, 58
Richard-Ginori, Società, 32
Rococo style, 18, 19, 22, 24, 36, 49, 51, 53, 54, 60
Rome, 63, 64
Rossetti, G. G., 29
Rouen porcelain, 7
Rudolstadt, 44
Ruzzini, Carlo, Doge, 8, 9, 14

Saint-Cloud porcelain, 19
Saint-Yrieix, kaolin from, 37
San Donato, 33
Schepers, Carlos, 52, 54, 57
Schepers, Gaetano, 46, 52
Schepers, Livio Ottavio, 46
Schepers, Sebastian, 52, 53
Seuter family of Augsburg, 50
Sèvres, influence, 18, 19, 48, 53, 56, 57
Sisto, Nicolo, 4
Soldani-Benzi, M., 32, 38, 40, 42
Sorrentino, Antonio, 63

star, mark, 21, 24, 33, 37, 68, 71
Stölzel, S., 9
Strasburg, 29–31
Sureda, Bartolomé, 53, 57, 72

Tacca, Pietro, 32, 43
Taglioni, Filippo, 59, 61, 62
Tamietti, Carlo, 31
tin-glaze, 34, 37, 60, 62
Tintoretto, 18
Tolerazzi, Fortunato, 16
Torre, Giuseppe della, 47
Tretto, clay from, 16, 20
Treviso, 15, 27
Tucci, Gaetano, 59
Turin, 29, 69
Turkish pottery, 3, 5, 6
turquoise ground, 48

Udine, 14
Urbino, 3, 5

'V' mark, 16, 67
'V' and cross, mark, 10, 66
'Va' mark, 10, 66
Varion, Jean-Pierre, 15, 20, 23, 25, 26
Vasari, Giorgio, 3
'Vena' mark, 10, 66
Venice, 1, 8
Venice, porcelain, 9–20, 66–8
Venuti, Domenico, 59, 61
Veronese, Paolo, 18
Vezzi family, 8, 9
Vicenza, clay from, 4, 16, 17, 20
Vicenza porcelain, 28
Vienna, influence, 9, 13, 33, 34, 35, 41, 50, 51, 59
Vincennes, 22, 25, 30
Vinovo, 29, 31, 69
Vische, 29, 69
Volpato, Giovanni, 64

Wagner, Anton, 29, 46
Wedgwood, influence, 40, 56, 58

1. *Medici porcelain, Florence, 1575–87.*
A. *Unmarked. Ht. 7⅝ in.*
B. *Mark, 'F' and the dome. D. 9⅝ in.*
Victoria and Albert Museum
(*See p. 5*)

2. *Medici porcelain, Florence, 1575–87.*
A. *Mark, 'F' and the dome. Ht. 7¼ in.*
Oxford, Ashmolean Museum
B. *Mark, 'F' and the dome. Ht. 8⅛ in.*
New York, Metropolitan Museum
C. *Mark, 'Prova'. Ht. 10⅞ in. Paris, Musée du Louvre*
(*See pp. 5, 6*)

3. *Medici porcelain, Florence, 1575–87.*
A. *No mark. Ht. 6 in.*
B. *Mark, 'F' and the dome. Ht. 6⅝ in.*
Victoria and Albert Museum
C. *Mark, 'F' and the dome. Ht. 11¼ in.*
Paris, Baronne Edouard de Rothschild
(See p. 5)

4A, B (*back*). *Probably Padua. Dated 1638. D. 4 in.*
Victoria and Albert Museum
C. *Medici porcelain, 1575–87. Mark, 'F' and the dome. D. 14⅝ in.*
Lisbon, Museu Nacional
(*See pp. 5, 6, 7*)

5. *Venice, Vezzi Factory, 1720–7.*
Painted in underglaze blue and thin gilding.
Unmarked. Ht. 12¼ in.
Victoria and Albert Museum
(See p. 11)

6. *Venice, Vezzi Factory, 1720–7.*
A. *In underglaze blue. Mark, 'Venezia'. Ht.* $4\frac{1}{2}$ *in.*
Sèvres, Musée Céramique
B. *In colours. No mark. Ht. about 9 in.*
Turin, Museo Civico
(See pp. 10, 11)

7. *Venice, Vezzi Factory, 1720–7. Painted in colours.*
A. *Marks 'V:ᵃ' in red and 'N', 'A' incised. Ht. 5¼ in.*
Sèvres, Musée Céramique
B. *Mark 'Ven.ᵃ' in red. Ht. 9 in.*
Venice, Fondazione Querini Stampaglia
(See pp. 10, 11, 12)

8. *Venice, Vezzi Factory, 1720–7.*
A. *Unmarked. Ht. 3 in. Cambridge, Fitzwilliam Museum*
B. *Marks incised, 'Ven^a' and 'A' on cup; 'Ven^a' on saucer.*
Ht. of cup 3 in. British Museum
C. *Marks 'A' and 'C' incised. Ht. 5⅞ in.*
Mr. Simon Goldblatt
(See pp. 10, 11, 13)

9. *Venice, Vezzi Factory, 1720–7.*
A. *In colours. Ht.* 3⅜ *in. Venice, Corror Museum*
B. *In colours. Unmarked. Ht.* 4⅜ *in.*
Victoria and Albert Museum
C. *Painted and marked in gold 'Ven^a'. Ht.* 4½ *in.*
British Museum
(*See pp.* 11, 12)

10. *Venice, Vezzi Factory, 1720–7.*
A. *Painted in blue enamel and gilt. Unmarked. Ht.* $3\frac{1}{4}$ *in.*
B. *Painted in red. Mark, 'Ven^a' and 'P' in red. Ht.* 3 *in.*
Both, Victoria and Albert Museum
C. *Painted in crimson and signed by Lodovico Ortolani. D.* $5\frac{1}{8}$ *in.*
British Museum
(*See pp. 10, 11, 12*)

11. *Venice, Vezzi Factory, 1720–7. Painted in colours.*
A. *Mark, 'Ven^a' in red. Ht. 3¼ in.*
B. *Marks, 'Ven^a' in red and 'MC' incised. D. 4½ in.*
Turin, Museo Civico
C. *Marks, 'Ven^a' in red and 'A' incised. Ht. 6 in.*
(A *and* C *Victoria and Albert Museum*)
(*See pp. 10, 11, 12*)

12. *Venice, Vezzi Factory, 1720–7.*
A. *In gold, red and black. D. about 7 in. Earl Spencer*
B. *In colours. Marks, 'A' and 'S' incised. D. 4⅞ in.*
Mr. Simon Goldblatt
(*See pp.* 10, 12)

13. *Venice, Vezzi Factory, 1720–7. Painted in colours.*
A. *Unmarked. Ht. 5¾ in.*
Victoria and Albert Museum
B. *Mark, 'Venᵃ A.G. 1726' in red. D. 4½ in.*
Turin, Museo Civico (See pp. 10, 11, 12)

14. *Venice, Hewelcke Factory, 1761–3. Painted in colours.*
Marks 'V' incised and painted in red.
A. *D. of saucer,* $5\frac{1}{8}$ *in.*
B. *D. 5 in.*
C. *Ht.* $3\frac{3}{4}$ *in. Victoria and Albert Museum*
(See p. 16)

15. *Venice, Hewelcke Factory, 1761–3.*
A. *Dated 1763. Ht. 9 in.*
B. *Mark, 'V' incised and painted in red. Ht. 2⅝ in.*
British Museum
(See p. 16)

16. *Venice, Cozzi Factory.*
A, B. *Painted in iron-red. Mark, anchor in red.*
Dated 1767. Ht. 8½ in. and 3¼ in.
Venice. Correr Museum

(*See p.* 18)

17. *Venice, Cozzi Factory. Painted in colours.*
Marks, an anchor in red. About 1770.
A. *Ht. 8⅜ in. Victoria and Albert Museum*
B. *Ht. 4 in. Former C. W. Heneage Collection*
(See p. 18)

18. *Venice, Cozzi Factory.*
A. *Unmarked. About 1765. Ht. 7¾ in. Italian Collection*
B. *Marked '1765 Venezia Fabᵃ Geminiano Cozzi' in red.*
Ht. 6⅝ in. British Museum
C. *Mark, anchor in red, about 1770. Ht. about 8 in.*
Turin, Museo Civico
(See p. 18)

19. *Venice, Cozzi Factory. Marks, an anchor in red.*
A. *About 1765–70. Ht. 4 in. Lord Phillimore*
B. *About 1770–80. W. 10½ in. Signora Campanini-Rovera*
(*See p. 18*)

20. *Venice, Cozzi Factory. Marks, an anchor in red.*
A, B. *About 1770–90. Ht. 4 and* $6\frac{5}{8}$ *in.*
C. *About 1765. D.* $8\frac{1}{4}$ *in. Victoria and Albert Museum*
(See p. 18)

21. *Venice, Cozzi Factory. Marks, an anchor in red or gold.*
A. *D. of saucer,* 4½ *in.* B. *D.* 4¾ *in. About* 1770.
C. *Signed 'F. Cozzi* 1780'. *D.* 9⅛ *in.*
Victoria and Albert Museum

(*See p.* 18)

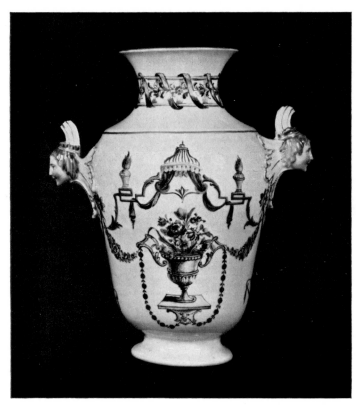

22. *Venice, Cozzi Factory. Marks, an anchor in red.*
A. *About 1770. D. of saucer, 4½ in. Mr. Simon Goldblatt*
B. *About 1790. Ht. 7½ in. Signore Sandro Orsi*
(*See p. 18*)

23. *Venice, Cozzi Factory. Marks, an anchor in red.*
About 1770–90.
A. *D. of saucer* 4⅞ *in.* B. *D.* 4¾ *in.* C. *D.* 9⅞ *in.*
Victoria and Albert Museum
(*See p.* 18)

24. *Venice, Cozzi Factory.*
A. *About 1780. Ht. 4½ in. and 5½ in. Signora Bonomi-Campanini*
B. *About 1770. Ht. about 5½ in. Senatore Aldo Crespi*
(*See p.* 19)

25. *Venice, Cozzi Factory. About* 1770–85.
A. *Ht.* 8 *in.* B. *Ht.* 7½ *in. Both Signore Sandro Orsi*
C. *Ht.* 3⅞ *in. Mr. S. Goldblatt.* D. *Ht.* 4 1/16 *in.,* E. 3⅞ *in.*
Victoria and Albert Museum
(*See p.* 19)

26. *Venice, Cozzi Factory.*
A. *About 1780. Ht. 9½ in. Conte Dino Barozzi*
B. *About 1780. Ht. 4½ in. Victoria and Albert Museum*
C. *About 1770. Ht. 4¾ in. Mr. Saul Levy*

(See p. 19)

27. *Venice, Cozzi Factory.*
A. *About 1770. Ht. 7 in. Signore Sandro Orsi*
B. *About 1800. Ht. 6⅝ in.*
C. *About 1790. Ht. 5½ in. Victoria and Albert Museum*
(*See p.* 19)

28. *Le Nove.*
A. *Marked GAB in monogram. About 1762. D. about 9 in.*
Sèvres, Musée Céramique
B. *About 1765–70. Ht. 5⅛ in. Victoria and Albert Museum*
(See pp. 20, 22)

29. *Le Nove. About 1765–70. Ht. 15½ in. Signore Sandro Orsi*
(See pp. 22, 24)

30. *Le Nove.*
A. *Mark, 'Nove' in relief. About 1765. Ht.* $5\frac{1}{4}$ *in.*
Victoria and Albert Museum
B. *About 1800. Ht.* $6\frac{1}{2}$ *in. Bisacco-Palazzi Collection*
(See pp. 22, 23)

31. *Le Nove. Signed 'NOVE. Gioni Marconi pinxt.' in gold.*
About 1800. *Ht.* 8¼ *in. Victoria and Albert Museum*
(*See p.* 23)

32. *Le Nove. Bowl and Stand. Signed 'MARCON pinse'.*
About 1785. D. of stand, 9¾ in. Bassano, Museo Civico
(See p. 23)

33. *Le Nove. Bowl and stand. Mark, a star in gold.*
About 1800. *D. of stand,* $9\frac{3}{4}$ *in.*
Bassano, Museo Civico
(*See pp.* 22, 23)

34. *Le Nove.*
A. *Mark, a star in red. About 1790. Ht.* $7\frac{1}{2}$ *in.*
Victoria and Albert Museum
B. *Mark, 'IF' monogram and a star in gold.*
C. *Mark, a star in gold. About 1800–20. D. of saucers* $4\frac{5}{8}$ *in.*
Cambridge, Fitzwilliam Museum
(See pp. 22, 23)

35. *Le Nove. Marked, 'G. B. NOVE'. About* 1810. *Ht.* 13¾ *in.*
Victoria and Albert Museum
(*See pp.* 23, 24)

36. *Le Nove. About* 1781–1800.
A. *Ht. 7 in. Signore Sandro Orsi*
B. *Ht. 6 in. Victoria and Albert Museum*
(*See p.* 24)

37. *Le Nove. About* 1781–1800.
A. *Mark, 'Nove' incised. Ht.* 9½ *in. British Museum*
B. *Ht.* 4¾ *in. Prof. Nino Barbantini*
C. *Ht.* 5½ *in. Milan, Museo Civico*
(*See p.* 24)

38. *Le Nove. Mark, 'Nove' incised. Dated 1789. Ht.* 10⅛ *in.*
Victoria and Albert Museum
(*See pp.* 21, 25)

39. *Le Nove. About* 1810. *Ht. about* 10 *in.*
Hamburg, Museum für Kunst und Gewerbe
(*See p.* 24)

40. *Este. The Virgin marked 'ESTE', St. John marked 'ESTE 1783'*
incised on the back. Ht. 15¼ in. and 15½ in.
Victoria and Albert Museum
(See p. 26)

41. *Este. About 1785.*
A. *Venus and Vulcan. Biscuit porcelain. Ht. 5¾ in.*
Victoria and Albert Museum
B. *Venus appearing to Aeneas and Achates. Ht. 8 in.*
Turin, Museo Civico
(*See p. 26*)

42. *Este. About* 1785.

A. *Ht. about 7 in. Hamburg, Museum für Kunst und Gewerbe*

B. *Ht.* $8\frac{7}{8}$ *in. Mr. Simon Goldblatt*

(*See pp.* 26, 27)

43. *Vinovo. About* 1779.
A. *Ht. about* 8 *in.*
B. *Ht. about* 5 *in. Turin, Museo Civico*
(*See pp.* 30, 31)

44. *Doccia. Painted in underglaze blue. About* 1740–5.
A. *Ht. about* $6\frac{1}{2}$ *in. Cav. A. Villoresi*
B. *Ht.* $9\frac{7}{8}$ *in. Marchese Roberto Venturi-Ginori*
(*See p.* 34)

45. *Doccia. Painted in underglaze blue. About* 1740–5.
A. *Ht.* 6⅜ *in.*
B. *D.* 10 *in. Victoria and Albert Museum*
(See p. 34)

46. *Doccia. About* 1746.
A. *Probably painted C. W. Anreiter. D. of saucer* $5\frac{1}{4}$ *in.*
Victoria and Albert Museum
B. *Probably painted by A. Anreiter. D.* 11 *in.*
Turin, Museo Civico
(*See pp.* 34, 35)

47. *Doccia, about* 1750–55.
A. *D.* 9¾ *in. Dr. S. Ducret*
B. *W.* 11 *in. Turin, Museo Civico*
(*See p.* 35)

48. Doccia. About 1755. Ht. 11 in.
Victoria and Albert Museum
(See p. 34)

49. *Doccia.*
A. *About 1755–8. Ht. 4½ in.*
B. *and* C. *About 1760–70. D. of saucers, 5 in. and 5¼ in.*
Victoria and Albert Museum
(*See pp. 34, 35, 36*)

50. *Doccia. Tin-glazed.*
A. *About 1770–80. D. of stand* $9\frac{1}{4}$ *in.*
B. *About 1770. D. of stand* $9\frac{1}{4}$ *in.*
Victoria and Albert Museum
(*See pp.* 36, 44)

51. *Doccia. Tin-glazed.*
A. *Signed 'G. B. F. 1785' in gold. D. of stand 9½ in.*
Victoria and Albert Museum
B. *About 1770. Ht. about 7½ in. Ginori Collection*
(*See p. 37*)

52. *Doccia. Tin-glazed.*
A. *About 1780–90. D. 9½ in. Victoria and Albert Museum*
B. *About 1790–1800. Ht. 8 in.*
Bedford, Cecil Higgins Museum
(*See pp. 20, 37, 44*)

53. *Doccia.*
A. *Tin-glazed. About* 1780–90. *D.* 9¾ *in.*
B. *About* 1792–1800. *Marks 'F' incised, the sign for tin,*
and a star in red. Ht. 6½ *in. Victoria and Albert Museum*
(See p. 37)

54. *Doccia. About* 1750–60. *Ht.* 12½ *in.*
Victoria and Albert Museum
(*See p.* 38)

55. *Doccia.*
A. *About* 1760 *or later. D. of saucer* 5 *in.*
B. *Mark, a crowned 'N', impressed. About* 1870. *Ht.* $4\frac{5}{8}$ *in.*
Victoria and Albert Museum
(*See pp.* 38, 39, 40)

56. *Doccia. About* 1745–55.
From a model of 1695 *by Massimiliano Soldani-Benzi.*
Ht. 21⅝*in. Marchese Roberto Venturi Ginori*
(*See pp.* 37, 38, 43)

57. *Doccia. About 1760–70. Ht.* $14\frac{1}{2}$ *in.*
Victoria and Albert Museum
(*See p. 38*)

58. *Doccia. About 1770. Ht. about 2 ft. 6 in.*
Ginori Collection, Florence
(*See p.* 43)

59. *Doccia.*
The Deposition, from a model by Massimiliano Soldani-Benzi.
About 1770. Ht. 11 in. British Museum
(See p. 43)

60. *Doccia*.
A, B. *About 1760–70. Ht. 4¼in. and 3⅞ in.*
Victoria and Albert Museum
C. *About 1750–60. Ht. about 7 in. Turin, Museo Civico*
(*See p.* 41)

61. *Doccia, about 1760–80.*

A, B. *Both, ht. 6 in. Victoria and Albert Museum*

C. *Ht. about 5 in. Hamburg Museum*

D. *Ht. about 5 in. Stockholm, National Museum*

(*See pp.* 41, 43)

62. *Doccia.*

A. *About* 1770. *Ht.* 8 *in. British Museum*

(*See p.* 42)

B. *Ht.* 5¼ *in. About* 1780–90. *Victoria and Albert Museum*

63. *Doccia.*

A. *About 1760–70. Ht. 3½ in. and 3⅛ in. Mrs. W. W. Winkworth*
B. *Ht. 9½ in. About 1790. Bedford, Cecil Higgins Museum*
(*See pp. 36, 41, 42*)

64. *Capodimonte. Mark, a fleur-de-lis in blue.*
A. *About 1745–50. D. of saucer 5½ in.*
Cambridge, Fitzwilliam Museum
B. *About 1750. D. of saucer 5¼ in.*
Victoria and Albert Museum
(See pp. 47, 48)

65. *Capodimonte. Mark, a fleur-de-lis in blue.*
A. *About* 1750. *D. of saucer* $5\frac{1}{4}$ *in.*
B. *About* 1745–50. *D. of saucer* $5\frac{1}{4}$ *in. Victoria and Albert Museum*
(*See pp.* 47, 48)

66. *Capodimonte. Mark, a fleur-de-lis in gold. About* 1745–50.
Ht. 8½ *in. Victoria and Albert Museum*
(See pp. 47, 48)

67. *Capodimonte.*
A, B. *About 1745–50. Mark, a blue fleur-de-lis. Ht. 2¾ in.*
C. *From same service as Plate 66. Ht. 4¾ in.*
Victoria and Albert Museum
(*See pp.* 47, 48)

68. *Capodimonte. Mark, a blue fleur-de-lis. About* 1750.
Ht. 10½ *in. Victoria and Albert Museum*
(See pp. 47, 48)

69. *Capodimonte. Mark, a fleur-de-lis in blue. About* 1750.
Ht. 13 *in. Victoria and Albert Museum*
(*See pp.* 47, 48)

70. *Capodimonte. About* 1750. *Mark, a blue fleur-de-lis.*
A. *In purple monochrome and gold. Ht.* $5\frac{1}{4}$ *in.*
Victoria and Albert Museum
B. *In colours. W. 8 in. Cambridge, Fitzwilliam Museum*
(*See pp.* 47, 48)

71. *Capodimonte. About 1750.*
A. *Mark, fleur-de-lis in blue. D.* 5$\frac{1}{2}$ *in.*
B. *Unmarked. About 1750. Ht. 4 in.*
Victoria and Albert Museum
(See pp. 47, 48)

72. *Capodimonte. About 1757–9. Marks, a blue fleur-de-lis.*
A. *Ht. 7 in. Dr. S. Ducret*
B. *W. 14 in. Madrid, Inst. de Valencia di Don Juan*
(See pp. 47, 49)

73. *Capodimonte. About 1757–9. Marks, a blue fleur-de-lis.*
A. *D.* 10 in. *Victoria and Albert Museum*
B. *D.* 10⅝ *in. Formerly Mr. C. W. Heanage*
(See pp. 47, 49, 56)

74. *Capodimonte. About* 1750. *Marks, a blue fleur-de-lis.*
A. *Ht.* 10¾ *in. Bedford, Cecil Higgins Museum*
B, C. *Ht.* 11 *in. Earl Spencer*
(*See p.* 47)

75. *Capodimonte.*
A, B. *About* 1750. *Ht.* $3\frac{1}{4}$ *in. and* $3\frac{7}{8}$ *in.*
Victoria and Albert Museum and formerly Mr. R. W. M. Walker
C. *About* 1758–9. *Ht.* $8\frac{1}{4}$ *in.*
New York, Hispanic Society of America
(*See pp.* 47, 49)

76. *Capodimonte. About 1750.*
A. *Mark, fleur-de-lis impressed. Ht.* $6\frac{5}{8}$ *in.*
B. *Mark, blue fleur-de-lis. Ht.* $5\frac{1}{2}$ *in.*
Victoria and Albert Museum

(*See p.* 50)

77. *Capodimonte. About* 1750. *Unmarked.*
A. *Ht.* 7½ *in.*
B. *Ht.* 7 *in. Milan, Museo Teatrale alla Scala*
(*See p.* 50)

78. *Capodimonte. About 1755. Mark, fleur-de-lis impressed.*
Ht. 18 in. Mr. J. B. Perret
(See p. 51)

79. *Capodimonte. About 1745–50. Ht.* 12½ *in.*
Milan, Museo Teatrale alla Scala
(See p. 50)

80. *Capodimonte. About 1750.*
A. *Mark, fleur-de-lis in blue.*
B, C. *Impressed. Hts. 5½in., 5½ in., 5⅞ in.*
Victoria and Albert Museum
D. *Ht. 6 in. Mr. Simon Goldblatt*
(*See pp. 50, 51*)

81. *Capodimonte, 1757–9.*
Detail of porcelain room from Portici.
Naples, Palazzodi Capodimonte
(*See pp.* 49, 51)

82. *Capodimonte or Buen Retiro. About 1758–65. Ht. about 9 in.*
Madrid, Museo Arqueologico Nacional
(See p. 51)

83. *Buen Retiro. About 1760–5. Ht. about 9 in.*
Earl Spencer
(See p. 54)

84. *Buen Retiro, 1760–5. Detail of porcelain room at Aranjuez.*
(*See p. 53*)

85. *Buen Retiro. About 1770–80.*
Detail of porcelain room in Royal Palace, Madrid
(See p. 54)

86. *Buen Retiro.*
A, B. *About 1765–70. Ht.* $7\frac{1}{2}$ *in. and* $6\frac{1}{2}$ *in.*
Madrid, Museo Municipal
C. *About 1770. Ht.* $6\frac{7}{8}$ *in.*
Madrid, Museo Arqueologico Nacional
(*See pp.* 54, 55)

87. *Buen Retiro. About* 1770–85. *Ht.* 12 *in.*
Madrid, Museo Arqueologico Nacional
(*See p.* 55)

88. *Buen Retiro. Mark, a blue fleur-de-lis.*
A. *About 1780–90. D. 8¾ in.*
B. *About 1760–70. Ht. 5¾ in.*
Victoria and Albert Museum
(*See pp. 49, 57*)

89. *Buen Retiro.*
A. *About 1790. Unmarked. Ht.* $9\frac{7}{8}$ *in.*
Victoria and Albert Museum
B. *After 1775. Mark, blue fleur-de-lis. W.* 10 *in.*
Madrid, Museo Arqueologico Nacional
(*See p.* 55)

90. *Naples. Marks, 'F.R.F.' crowned, in blue.*
A. *Dated 1772. D.* 5½ *in. Turin, Museo Civico*
B. *About 1780. Ht.* 5⅛ *in.*
Victoria and Albert Museum
(*See p. 60*)

91. *Naples. About 1773–80.*
A. *Mark 'F.R.F.' crowned, in red. D. about 9 in.*
B. *Same mark in blue. W. about 10 in. Turin, Museo Civico*
(*See p.* 60)

92. *Naples. Unmarked.*
A. *About* 1800. *D.* 9⅜ *in.*
B. *About* 1785–95. *D.* 10½ *in.*
Victoria and Albert Museum
(*See pp.* 60, 61)

93. *Naples.*

A. *Mark, crowned 'N' in blue. About 1800–6. Ht. 6¾ in.*
B. *Tin-glazed. Mark, 'F.R.F.' crowned, in red. About 1785–95.*
D. 10¼ in. Victoria and Albert Museum

(*See p. 96*)

94. *Naples. Unmarked.*
A. *About 1795. Ht.* $5\frac{1}{8}$ *in.*
B. *About 1780. Ht. 6 in.*
C. *Biscuit porcelain. About 1795. Ht. 7 in.*
Victoria and Albert Museum
(*See pp.* 60, 63)

95. *Naples.*
A, B. *Unmarked. About 1780. Ht. 4¾ in. and 4⅞ in.*
Victoria and Albert Museum
C. *Crowned 'N' mark in blue. Ht. 8 in.*
Cambridge, Fitzwilliam Museum
(See pp. 60, 63)

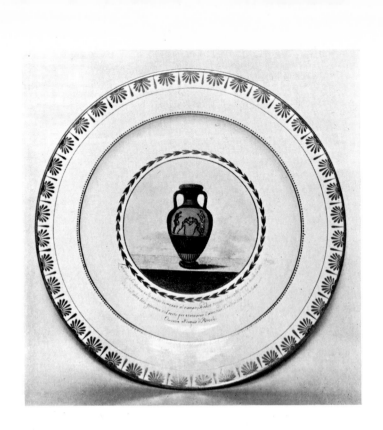

96. *Naples. Service sent to King George III in 1787.*
A. *Tin-glazed. D. 9¼ in.*
B. *Ht. 8¾ in. Windsor Castle*
(See p. 62)